Space, Stars, and the Beginning of Time

What the Hubble Telescope Saw

Elaine Scott

CLARION BOOKS · HOUGHTON MIFFLIN HARCOURT · BOSTON NEW YORK · 2011 ·

▶ **CLARION BOOKS:**

215 Park Avenue South, New York, NY 10003

Copyright © 2011 by Elaine Scott
The text was set in 13-point Scala.
Book design by Sharismar Rodriguez
All rights reserved.

For information about permission to reproduce selections from this book, write to Permissions, Houghton Mifflin Harcourt Publishing Company, 215 Park Avenue South, New York, New York 10003.

www.hmhbooks.com

Clarion Books is an imprint of Houghton Mifflin Harcourt Publishing Company.

▶ **LIBRARY OF CONGRESS CATALOGING-IN-PUBLICATION DATA:**

Scott, Elaine.

Space, stars, and the beginning of time : what the Hubble telescope saw / by Elaine Scott.

p. cm.

ISBN 978-0-547-24189-0

1. Hubble Space Telescope (Spacecraft)—Juvenile literature. I. Title.

QB500.268.S364 2011

522'.2919—dc22

2010008040

On the title page: The Hubble reveals galaxy NGC1672, more than 60,000 million light-years away from Earth. Star-forming clouds and dark bands of interstellar dust appear along the edges of the galaxy's spiral arms.

On the contents page: The gorgeous, winding arms of galaxy NGC5194 are actually long lanes of stars and gas laced with dust. The galaxy's face-on view allows astronomers to use Hubble images to study this classic spiral galaxy's structure and star formation processes. To the far right is another galaxy, NGC5195.

BOTH: NASA, ESA, AND THE HUBBLE HERITAGE TEAM (STScI/AURA)–ESA/HUBBLE COLLABORATION.

Manufactured in China

LEO 10 9 8 7 6 5 4 3 2 1

4500226790

ACKNOWLEDGMENTS

No book is ever written by the author alone, and this one is no exception. I want to thank my editor, Jennifer Greene, whose wise queries made this a far better manuscript than it might have been without them. Zolt Levay of the Space Telescope Science Institute was wonderfully helpful with the picture research and Cheryl Gundy, also of STScI, has been a steady support as I have written all my books on space and the Hubble. Dr. Laura Danley graciously answered my questions years ago, and now as well. I'm saving the last accolade for Dr. Mario Livio, senior astrophysicist at STScI. I continue to be stunned that this brilliant, distinguished scholar took time from his demanding schedule to read the manuscript and correct the errors he found.

I am deeply grateful to all of you.
—E.S.

FOR JACKSON SCOTT BEASLEY,
WHO WAS BORN MARCH 19, 2009,
AND IS THE BRIGHTEST STAR IN MY UNIVERSE.

WITH LOVE FROM GIGI

CONTENTS

INTRODUCTION   1

ONE:
THE SPYGLASS GROWS UP   7

TWO:
A FINAL VISIT TO THE HUBBLE   15

THREE:
THE BEGINNING OF TIME   21

FOUR:
THE DARK FORCES AND BLACK HOLES   29

FIVE:
THE LIFE CYCLE OF A STAR   39

SIX:
RECIPE FOR A PLANET   45

AFTERWORD   53

GLOSSARY   60

FOR FURTHER READING   63

INDEX   64

INTRODUCTION

HAVE YOU EVER wished you could travel back in time? Or visit another planet? Or see a star close up? Have you ever wondered about the mysteries of the universe, and whether other life-forms, similar to humans, exist somewhere? These are important questions that people have been asking for hundreds of years. Throughout those years many books—fact and fiction—have been written as authors and readers seek answers to the questions they have.

Perhaps one of the most beloved tales about travel to distant galaxies is Madeleine L'Engle's novel *A Wrinkle in Time*. It tells the story of Meg Murry, her little brother, Charles Wallace, and their friend Calvin, who go on a mysterious journey through the universe in search of the Murry children's father, who has vanished from planet Earth. When Mrs. Murry tries to explain Mr. Murry's sudden disappearance, Meg asks her mother, "Do you think things always have an explanation?"

Mrs. Murry replies that she believes they do, but goes on to say,

Two spiral galaxies almost collide in space. The larger galaxy's energy has distorted the shape of the smaller one, causing it to fling out long streamers of stars and gas that stretch out a distance of a hundred thousand light-years.
NASA, ESA, AND THE HUBBLE HERITAGE TEAM (STScI)

"With our human limitations, we're not always able to understand the explanations. But you see, Meg, just because we don't understand doesn't mean that the explanation doesn't exist."

Meg answers, "I like to understand things."

Like Meg, many of us want to understand things, even if the topics are difficult ones—like space, time, and the mysteries of the universe. To understand anything we must ask questions. Madeleine L'Engle was no exception; she liked to ask questions, too. In her introduction to *A Wrinkle in Time,* she asks her readers: "If anyone invited you to go to a newly discovered galaxy, would you go?" How would you answer? *Would* you go? Would you be frightened? Excited? Curious? Without the aid of a telescope, you can look up into the night sky and see a few of the planets in our solar system and thousands of stars. With a telescope, we are able to see billions of stars, and astronomers have detected hundreds of planets orbiting in solar systems beyond our own. Many wonder, is Earth *really* the only planet that supports life? What do you think other planets would be like?

Madeleine L'Engle used fiction—made-up characters and a made-up story—to explore important questions about the universe. Occasionally a novel, such as *A Wrinkle in Time,* becomes meaningful for generations of readers. Likewise, a scientific instrument can become so important, so useful, its contributions to science so amazing, that it changes the way people look at themselves and their world. The Hubble Space Telescope is that kind of instrument. It has changed the way we understand the universe and Earth's place in it.

Named for the great twentieth-century astronomer Edwin

The Hubble's instruments captured this image of a cloud of space dust and gas that surrounds a giant star at the outer edge of the Milky Way galaxy.
NASA AND THE HUBBLE HERITAGE TEAM (AURA/STScI)

The Hubble Space Telescope orbits high above Earth's atmosphere, returning spectacular images of the universe to Earth. **STScI**

THE HUBBLE SPACE TELESCOPE

▶ **LAUNCHED:** April 24, 1990

▶ **LENGTH:** 43.5 feet, about the size of a school bus

▶ **WEIGHT:** 24,500 pounds

▶ **COST AT LAUNCH:** $1.5 billion

▶ **POWER SOURCE:** the Sun

▶ **POWER STORAGE:** Energy from the Sun is stored in 6 nickel-hydrogen batteries, equal to 20 car batteries

▶ **TIME TO COMPLETE ONE EARTH ORBIT:** 97 minutes

Hubble (1889–1953), the Hubble Space Telescope has been called one of the greatest scientific instruments of all time. The information it has returned to astronomers and other scientists around the world—each and every *week*—is enough to fill a 3,600-foot-long bookshelf. That's the length of ten football fields laid out end to end! Cameras onboard this great observatory photograph new stars as they are born, and old stars as they die. Images reveal massive black holes from which nothing, not even light, can escape. The Hubble has detected new planets orbiting other stars, proving that our solar system with its eight planets isn't the only solar system in the universe. Scientists have known about gravity, the force that attracts, or pulls, objects with mass toward each other, since Isaac Newton (1643–1727) first wrote about it. Recently, astronomers have used the Hubble to reveal another mystery, dark energy, which exerts a force that appears to be pulling things apart.

This remarkable telescope shows us not only what is happening in the universe now, but also what has happened in the past. The Hubble can retrieve data from billions of years ago, almost to the moment the universe was born in a massive explosion known as the Big Bang. Knowing what has happened in the past can help scientists determine what may happen in the future.

Like any instrument, the Hubble Space Telescope has needed maintenance throughout the years. Servicing the Hubble is dangerous and expensive work. However, during the time it has been in orbit, teams of spacewalking astronauts have competed for the privilege of making the trip to the space observatory. On May 11, 2009, a crew of seven astronauts launched into space from

Cape Canaveral to service the Hubble for the fifth and final time, improving its capabilities and making necessary repairs. Four of the astronauts would be the last human beings to touch the telescope.

As he anticipated the final mission to the Hubble, Mission Commander Scott Altman said, "Hubble puts cutting-edge science together with a visual image that grabs the public's imagination. I think that's the first step in exploration . . . it's like taking you on a journey thirteen and a half billion light-years away, while you sit there at home and look out at the universe."

Before the Hubble was launched, there were many things about space, time, and our universe that astronomers, physicists, and other scientists didn't understand. But just as Mrs. Murry told Meg, it didn't mean there were no explanations to be found. The great physicist Albert Einstein (1879–1955) once said, "The important thing is not to stop questioning." During the twenty years it has been in orbit, the Hubble Space Telescope has provided many explanations about questions scientists have had about the universe. Of course, for every question it has answered, it has raised more, which is not a bad thing. Scientists believe that explanations for the mysteries of the universe exist and, therefore, it is always possible to find answers. Dr. Laura Danly, an astrophysicist who worked with the Hubble Space Telescope and is now curator at the Griffith Observatory in Los Angeles, California, said, "It annoys me when people talk about 'the secrets of the universe.' The universe doesn't have secrets. It reveals itself to us." The Hubble Space Telescope helps us see what those revelations are.

Earth, Moon, and the Hubble. Galileo studied the Moon with his telescope, but he probably could not have imagined a telescope that would take pictures of the Moon from space. STS-103 CREW AND NASA

ONE

THE SPYGLASS GROWS UP

Hans Lippershey (LIP-er-shy) (1570–1619), a Dutch optician, is credited with the invention of the telescope in 1608. Lippershey held two lenses in front of each other and discovered that objects viewed through both lenses appear larger and closer than they actually are. Since it is inconvenient to hold a lens in each hand for any length of time, Lippershey mounted them on either end of a long tube, thus creating the telescope. Lippershey wanted the Dutch government to give him a pension in exchange for his telescope, but because there were a few other people who claimed the telescope as their invention, the government refused to give Lippershey either a pension or a patent. But the Dutch government did pay him 900 florins, roughly $360. In 1608, that was a large sum of money. The Dutch used the telescope to spy on enemy ships that approached by sea, so Lippershey's invention became known as a "spyglass." Once scientists began to use the instru-

The Hubble captured this display of starlight, glowing gas, and dark clouds of interstellar dust in Galaxy NGC 1300. Blue and red giant stars can be seen in its spiral arms.

NASA, ESA, and the Hubble Heritage Team (STScI)

A painting by Vincenzo Cesare Cantagalli showing Galileo dictating his observations to his secretary.

THE ART ARCHIVE/CORBIS

ment, however, it became obvious that it was useful for much more than spying.

Word of Lippershey's invention quickly spread through Europe. In Italy, a scientist named Galileo Galilei (ga-luh-LAY-oh ga-luh-LAY-ee) (1564–1642) learned of it and decided to make his own. In 1609, Galileo made a telescope that was superior to Lippershey's; it was able to magnify an object up to twenty times its size, while Lippershey's device only magnified objects up to three times. Galileo used his instrument differently, too. Instead of using it to look out to sea, Galileo turned his telescope upright to look at the heavens. He discovered—among many other things—that Jupiter had four moons, and that the Milky Way was not just a smear of light in the night sky, but rather was made up of billions of stars densely packed together.

The telescope also helped Galileo make his most controversial discovery. Based on observations made through his spyglass, Galileo concluded that Nicolaus Copernicus (Co-PER-ni-cus) (1473–1543) had been correct in stating that the Sun is at the center of our solar system, not the Earth, as most people in those days believed. Galileo hypothesized that the planets moved in a circular orbit around the Sun. It was not until years later that Johannes Kepler (1571–1601) would use a telescope to determine that the planets move around the sun in an oval, or elliptical, orbit.

Galileo's telescope revolutionized astronomy, but the instrument and others like it had an annoying flaw. The images astronomers saw through those early telescopes had colored edges. In 1668, the great English scientist Isaac Newton, who is best known for his work with gravity and the laws of motion, figured out how

Using his telescope, Galileo discovered that Jupiter has four moons, but he could not have seen Jupiter and its moon Ganymede as clearly as the Hubble did on April 9, 2007. NASA/ESA AND E. KARKOSCHKA (UNIVERSITY OF ARIZONA)

to fix the problem. Newton had been working with prisms, and he realized that the colored edge was caused by light being refracted, or bent, as it passed through a telescope's lenses. Newton built a telescope that used a mirror to *reflect* the light rather than refract it. The colored edge disappeared, and the images cleared up. To-day, most telescopes use a combination of lenses and mirrors to capture light.

As years went by, more and more improvements were made to telescopes. But all telescopes, no matter how large or sophisticated, were Earth-bound, creating a difficulty that scientists couldn't im-prove by making further adjustments: astronomers still had to peer through Earth's atmosphere to view the night sky. Our atmosphere is made up of wiggling gases that hug our planet like the fuzz on a peach, and those gases can cause distortions in what the astron-omers can see. Stars are often described as twinkling or dancing

Continued from page 8.

▶ **TESTING:** Hypotheses must be tested by other scientists before they can be accepted. Other astronomers repeated Galileo's observations and calculations. Most accepted Galileo's hypothesis that the planets traveled in a circular orbit around the Sun.

▶ **THEORY:** When many scientists agree on a hypothesis, it becomes a theory. Once a hypothesis becomes a theory, scientists begin to accept the theory as true. Galileo's hypothesis of planetary motion became a theory and was considered true. Kepler's discoveries disproved Galileo's theory. Kepler formed a new hypothesis: the planets move in elliptical orbits. When no one was able to disprove Kepler's hypothesis, it became a theory.

▶ **LAW:** Eventually theories can become scientific laws, like Isaac Newton's laws of motion. A law in science is a theory that has been carefully investigated and tested over many years and is widely accepted as fact. It is important to realize, however, that scientific theories and even laws can change when or if new information that disproves them becomes available, just as Kepler's discovery about the planets' elliptical orbits replaced Galileo's theory.

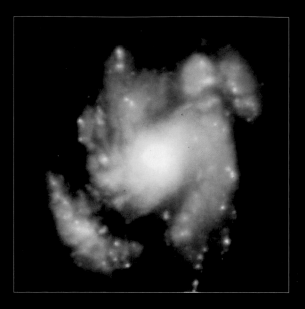

WIDE FIELD PLANETARY CAMERA 1

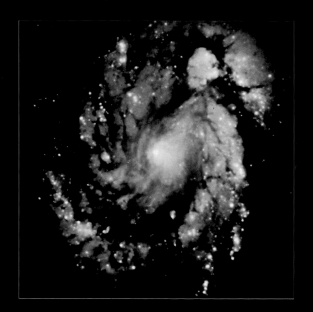

WIDE FIELD PLANETARY CAMERA 2

The defect in the Hubble's primary mirror, called a *spherical aberration*, made images appear out of focus and blurry. During the first servicing mission to the Hubble, astronauts installed a piece of new equipment called the Corrective Optics Space Telescope Axial Replacement, or COSTAR. Just as glasses fix out-of-focus vision in humans, COSTAR corrected the Wide Field Planetary Camera's fuzzy vision. Images show the core of galaxy M100 before the repair and after. STScI

(think "Twinkle, Twinkle, Little Star"), but in space, stars do not twinkle. They only twinkle if you see them from Earth. As long as scientists used telescopes on Earth, our planet's atmosphere would always be in the way.

The first astronomical satellite, Ariel 1, was launched by Great Britain in 1962. Telescopes had left Earth and moved to the sky. But these early satellites were small, and in most cases observed in only one wavelength of light. Then came the Hubble Space Telescope.

On April 24, 1990, the Hubble was carried into orbit. Unlike the previous satellites, the Hubble was a large instrument that would allow astronomers to observe in many different wavelengths of light. Scientists from around the world rejoiced at its launch. They eagerly anticipated what they might learn about our solar system and the universe as a whole.

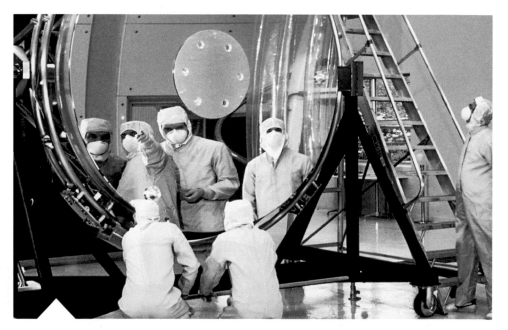

Before the Hubble's launch into space, technicians worked on its main mirror, which is eight feet in diameter. Light from an object enters the Hubble, reflects off this mirror, and hits a second, smaller mirror. The light then bounces back through a two-foot hole in the center of the main mirror where the Hubble's scientific instruments capture it. In this image, the hole is protected by a cover. The technicians are wearing masks and protective garments to prevent contamination of the telescope. NASA, 1990

The Hubble's cameras captured a star-forming region of space 210,000 light-years away, in a galaxy called the Small Magellanic Cloud. NASA/ESA AND A. NOTA (STScI/ESA)

▶ **WIDE FIELD CAMERA 3 (WFC3):**

This new camera will allow the Hubble to see deeper into space, and therefore farther back in time, than ever before. Light comes to us in different wavelengths. Young stars glow with ultraviolet light; but because the universe is expanding, the first stars and galaxies that formed after the birth of the universe are now so old and far away that their light is "redshifted," which means it only glows in the infrared wavelengths. This camera will be able to see and photograph ancient stars and galaxies that formed close to the beginning of time.

▶ **COSMIC ORIGINS SPECTROGRAPH (COS):**

A spectrograph is an optical instrument that studies objects that either absorb or produce light. The spectrograph can detect an object's electromagnetic spectrum, or the range of radiation it produces. The different types of radiation, from longest to shortest wave, include radio waves, microwaves, infrared light waves, visible light (the light we see), ultraviolet light, X-rays, and gamma rays, the shortest wavelength of all. The spectrograph works by breaking up light from an object into its individual wavelengths, so that the object's composition, temperature, motion, and other chemical and physical properties can be analyzed. The COS works mainly in the ultraviolet wavelength. Scientists will use this spectrograph to study how stars and galaxies formed and evolved over time. It will also help determine how some elements, like carbon and iron first came into being and have increased throughout the universe over time.

▶ **SPACE TELESCOPE IMAGING SPECTROGRAPH (STIS):**

Another spectrograph, this instrument was already installed on the Hubble, but needed repair. Before its failure in August 2004, STIS helped scientists discover and study supermassive black holes at the centers of other galaxies, and astronomers used it to analyze gases

The STIS is a general-purpose spectrograph that operates in the same way the COS does.

▶ **ADVANCED CAMERA FOR SURVEYS (ACS):**

Many of the Hubble's most amazing older images were taken with this camera, which suffered an electronic failure in January 2007. The camera was repaired on STS-125. The ACS will study large areas of the sky in both the visible and red wavelengths. Scientists will also use the ACS to unravel the mysteries of dark energy and dark matter.

▶ **FINE GUIDANCE SENSOR (FGS):**

This instrument locks on to a guide star, allowing the Hubble to remain precise and steady as it points toward an object.

▶ **GYROSCOPES:**

A gyroscope maintains direction and stability in moving objects such as planes, boats, and space telescopes. The Hubble has six gyroscopes and all six were replaced during the final mission. The FGS and gyroscopes give the Hubble the same level of precision as someone standing in Washington, D.C., with a laser beam, touching a dime someone else is holding in New York City!

▶ **THE SCIENCE INSTRUMENT COMMAND & DATA HANDLING MODULE (SI C & DH):**

SI C & DH is a computer and collection of electronic instruments that allows scientists on the ground to send commands to the Hubble in space. It also enables the telescope to send its information back to Earth.

▶ **BATTERIES:**

All of these instruments are powered by six batteries. The batteries receive their power from the telescope's two solar arrays, which gather energy from the Sun.

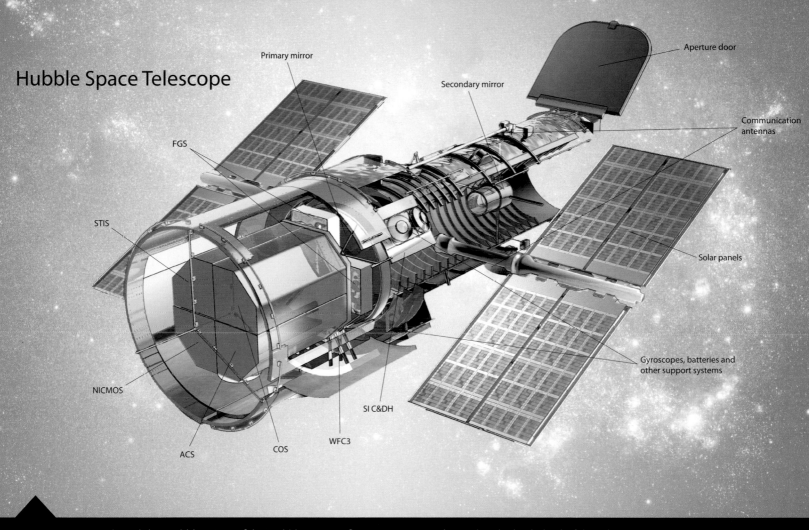

Hubble Space Telescope

Primary mirror

Secondary mirror

Aperture door

Communication antennas

FGS

STIS

Solar panels

NICMOS

Gyroscopes, batteries and other support systems

ACS

COS

WFC3

SI C&DH

Instruments onboard the Hubble. Most of the Hubble's scientific instruments are located in the back third of the telescope. ESA

THE HUBBLE'S PIPELINE TO EARTH

Light from the stars enters the telescope and is analyzed by its instruments. Then the data is sent to a relay satellite; from there the information goes to a ground station in White Sands, New Mexico, and on to Goddard Space Flight Center in Greenbelt, Maryland. The last stop for the data is the Space Telescope Science Institute in Baltimore, Maryland. STScI

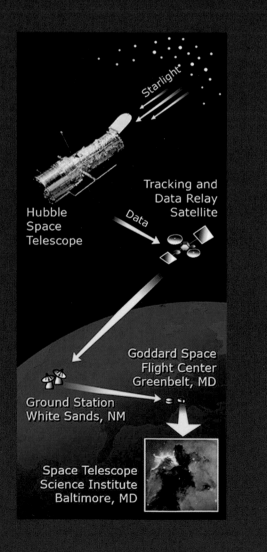

Starlight

Hubble Space Telescope

Data

Tracking and Data Relay Satellite

Goddard Space Flight Center Greenbelt, MD

Ground Station White Sands, NM

Space Telescope Science Institute Baltimore, MD

After all the excitement, the Hubble got off to a rocky start. The main mirror was ground incorrectly (by 1/50th of the thickness of a human hair!), so the telescope's ability to focus properly was severely limited. People who use eyeglasses can easily understand the Hubble's problem. A corrective lens in a pair of glasses or contact lenses focuses the light that comes through it, allowing the person wearing the lens to see clearly. If those lenses are incorrectly ground, the focus will be off and the person's vision will be blurry. In December 1993, the Hubble's vision problem was corrected during the first servicing mission to the telescope. Astronauts installed an instrument called the Corrective Optics Space Telescope Axial Replacement, or COSTAR for short. This instrument served as glasses for the Hubble, and soon thereafter, amazing images returned to Earth.

Astronauts have serviced the Hubble four more times since the first mission, installing new equipment and updating existing instruments each time. These missions are risky for the astronauts, they require years of training and planning, and each one costs hundreds of millions of dollars. However, the Hubble Space Telescope has allowed scientists to make discoveries about our universe that are, indeed, priceless, thanks to images that have been and continue to be shared around the world. According to the Space Telescope Science Institute, "The Hubble Space Telescope has had a major impact in every area of astronomy, from the solar system to objects at the edge of the universe."

TWO

A Final Visit to the Hubble

A LOT CAN GO wrong with a space flight—and many problems begin during launch. In 2003, the space shuttle *Columbia* was damaged during take off. As it ascended into space, debris struck and damaged part of the shuttle's heat shield. Nevertheless, the shuttle made it into orbit, and during the mission there weren't signs of serious problems. The astronauts onboard and Mission Control all thought things were going well. But *Columbia* had sustained damage beyond repair. The debris had torn a hole in a panel of the shuttle's left wing, so when *Columbia* made its fiery reentry into Earth's atmosphere, hot gases entered the wing and the shuttle broke up, killing all onboard. NASA immediately canceled all future shuttle missions while it investigated what had happened to *Columbia*. The final mission to the Hubble was among those canceled.

For a while, it looked as if the Hubble would never be serviced again. The observatory would be left in space, unrepaired—its use as a scientific instrument greatly lessened—and it would slowly fall apart. At the time, astronaut John Grunsfeld, who had made previous trips to the Hubble and had been scheduled to go on the final mission, said, "As a certified 'Hubble Hugger,' that hit me like a two-by-four. I just couldn't believe that we would prematurely make that decision."

He wasn't the only one who was disappointed. Scientists, students, teachers, and the general public cried out in protest. They could not imagine a world without the Hubble. At first, NASA stuck by its decision not to repair its famous telescope. Then the agency considered the possibility of sending robots to the Hubble instead of humans. But after careful consideration, that plan was laid aside. The telescope had been designed to be serviced by astronauts, not robots—astronauts who had trained for years to perform delicate work. Furthermore, some of the instruments onboard the Hubble had not been intended to be repaired at all, much less by robots. Captain Scott Altman saw additional value in sending astronauts on this mission. Astronauts would not only be more likely to successfully make the repairs the Hubble needed, they would also receive valuable training for future missions, when it will be important to make repairs in space. "I think it's a step that we need to take to make us better able to go to places like Mars," Altman said. "Being able to demonstrate this [repair] in space is a key element of us growing as a space-faring people."

Finally, in 2006, NASA announced that STS-125 would go forward. A crew of seven astronauts onboard *Atlantis* would head to the Hubble to service it one last time. John Grunsfeld, the "Hubble Hugger," would be the payload commander and make spacewalks

THE CREW

SCOTT ALTMAN, MISSION COMMANDER (D)

As mission commander Scott had overall responsibility for the safety and execution of the mission. He flew *Atlantis* to its rendezvous with the Hubble and was responsible for the operation of all the shuttle's systems. His duties included inspecting the heat shield for damage after the crew was in orbit.

GREGORY C. JOHNSON, PILOT (C)

In addition to piloting the shuttle, Gregory was the official photographer and charged with documenting the mission with an IMAX 3-D camera.

MICHAEL GOOD, MISSION SPECIALIST 1 (B)

Michael made the second and fourth spacewalks with Mike Massimino.

MEGAN MCARTHUR, MISSION SPECIALIST 2 (E)

Megan manipulated the robotic arm, getting the astronauts where they needed to be to service the telescope and performing other tasks.

JOHN GRUNSFELD, MISSION SPECIALIST 3 (F)

This was John's third trip to the Hubble and his fifth space flight. He was the lead spacewalker and conducted the first, third, and fifth spacewalks.

MIKE MASSIMINO, MISSION SPECIALIST 4 (A)

Mike made two spacewalks when the telescope was serviced in 2002, and two spacewalks with Michael Good on the final mission.

ANDREW "DREW" FEUSTEL, MISSION SPECIALIST 5 (G)

Drew performed the first, third, and fifth spacewalks with John Grunsfeld. This was his first space mission.

The crew of STS-125. The astronauts are wearing the training version of their orange launch and reentry garments. These pressure suits help astronauts withstand the stresses on their bodies as they break free of Earth's gravity on their launch into space, and as they feel its pull upon their return to Earth. NASA

Space shuttle *Atlantis* moments after its launch, carrying the crew of STS-125 to their rendezvous with the Hubble Space Telescope. **NASA**

with his partner Andrew Feustel. Mike Massimino and Michael Good would also make spacewalks. Megan McArthur would operate the robotic arm, and Gregory C. Johnson would pilot the shuttle. Scott Altman would lead them as mission commander.

Of course, the danger was still there. Even though NASA now understood what had happened to *Columbia,* something unexpected could always go wrong. But NASA had a plan to rescue the crew in the event of an emergency, and so the intense training began for the astronauts and for everyone on the ground who supports them.

It takes months, even years, to get one shuttle ready for a mission, but in an unprecedented move, NASA decided to prepare *two* shuttles for launch at Cape Canaveral. *Atlantis* would carry the crew to the Hubble, and *Endeavour* would be waiting on a nearby launch pad, ready to go, should the *Atlantis* crew need rescue.

On the fifth and final spacewalk of the mission, John Grunsfeld works on the Hubble. Note the yellow handrails that were installed all over the telescope in order to make it easier for astronauts to pull themselves around the observatory. A safety cable runs from Grunsfeld's right leg and is attached to a point on the shuttle, preventing him from floating away should he lose his grip on the handrail. **NASA**

Atlantis roared off the launch pad at 2:01 p.m. Eastern Daylight Time on May 11, 2009, as scheduled. Three days later, it caught up with the Hubble, which was orbiting Earth at 17,500 miles an hour. Once the shuttle and the Hubble were in the same orbit, Megan McArthur used the shuttle's robotic arm to capture the telescope and bring it safely to *Atlantis*'s cargo bay, the back portion of the space plane, open to space and used to carry equipment. Then in a series of five spacewalks that took place over five days, Drew Feustel, John Grunsfeld, Mike Massimino, and Michael Good began their work. In teams of two, the spacewalking astronauts installed Wide Field Camera 3, replaced all six of the Hubble's gyroscopes, installed the Cosmic Origins Spectrograph, and repaired the Advanced Camera for Surveys as well as the Space Telescope Imaging Spectrograph. Then they replaced batteries and sensors in order to keep the Hubble running for many years.

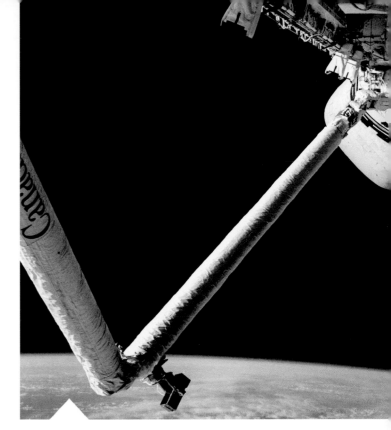

The space shuttle's robotic arm has two shoulder joints, one elbow joint, and three wrist joints and is 45 feet long. The arm is used to launch and retrieve satellites such as the Hubble and move astronauts around while they make spacewalks. It is also used in safety inspections. Sensors and cameras attached to the arm send information to the crew and to Mission Control, allowing experts to check the shuttle for any damage. **NASA**

On the outside, looking in. Michael Good peers through the window of *Atlantis* and greets crew members inside. Mike Massimino is in the background, on the left side of the shuttle's cargo bay. **NASA**

RESCUE IN SPACE

Most manned space flights go to the International Space Station, which is in continuous orbit around Earth. If a space shuttle was damaged, astronauts could take shelter there. But the Hubble Space Telescope is in orbit far away from the space station, and a crippled shuttle would not be able to make the journey there safely. Since it takes months, if not years, to get a shuttle ready to fly into space, and supplies onboard *Atlantis* support the crew of seven astronauts for three weeks, NASA prepared the shuttle *Endeavour,* too. Had something gone wrong with *Atlantis, Endeavour* and a reduced crew of four astronauts would have launched toward *Atlantis* within a week. Once *Endeavour* reached *Atlantis, Atlantis* would have used its robotic arm to latch on to *Endeavour.* With the two shuttles securely locked together, a series of spacewalks would have begun, and the seven-member crew from *Atlantis* would have slowly made its way to the safety of the replacement shuttle. With eleven astronauts onboard, *Endeavour* would have been a crowded shuttle as it made its way back to Earth!

Space shuttle *Atlantis* arrives at Edwards Air Force Base on May 24, 2009. Note the drag parachute on its tail, used to slow the vehicle down on the runway. The shuttle and its crew had made 197 orbits of Earth and traveled 5,276 million miles as the crew worked to repair the Hubble for the final time. **NASA**

Now that the job was complete, it was time for *Atlantis* to head back to Earth. Like all space shuttles, *Atlantis* is actually a space plane, complete with wings and landing gear. Although a shuttle is shot into space with a rocket, it returns to Earth as a powerless glider, rolling to a stop on a runway—usually at Cape Canaveral in Florida. Occasionally, the weather at Cape Canaveral makes it too dangerous for a shuttle to land there. In those cases, the spaceship can be rerouted to other landing sites in the United States or even other countries around the world. Because of potential storms in Florida, the crew had to remain in space for an extra two days, circling Earth. Finally, after making 197 orbits around Earth, covering 5,276 *million miles, Atlantis* and its crew landed safely at Edwards Air Force Base in California on May 24, 2009.

The mission was a complete success. The Hubble had been effectively serviced and repaired and was now capable of helping astronomers and cosmologists around the world explore deeper into space than ever before.

THREE

THE BEGINNING OF TIME

ASTRONOMY, one of the world's oldest sciences, is the observation and study of planets, stars, and galaxies. An astronomer is a scientist who practices astronomy. In a sense, the first humans were the first astronomers, since it is safe to assume they looked up into the night sky, gazing at the stars and the planets, surely wondering what they were. By 1300 B.C. the Chinese were recording their observations.

As time and science progressed, the field of astronomy grew, and other kinds of scientific study emerged, such as astrophysics. Astrophysics is concerned with the physics of the universe—its heat, light, and temperature, as well as the composition of stars, galaxies, and the interstellar medium (or the space between the stars and galaxies). An astrophysicist is a scientist who practices astrophysics.

Cosmology is the scientific study of the universe's origin, evolution, and ultimate fate. As a science, cosmology has existed

Albert Einstein in 1905, the year he published five papers, including his groundbreaking theory of relativity.
BETTMANN/CORBIS

for only approximately four hundred years. Following the invention of the telescope, astronomers, physicists, and other scientists have developed new theories that have been tested. While some theories have been disproved, others, such as Newton's laws of motion, have become scientific law. Occasionally, scientists will develop a theory and be surprised by the results of their own experiments. Allegedly, Albert Einstein did not believe his own theory of relativity, which suggested that our universe might be expanding. It took astronomer Edwin Hubble to prove to Einstein that his theory was correct.

Hubble arrived at the Mount Wilson Observatory in Pasadena, California, in 1919 to work with the Hooker Telescope, which was then the largest telescope in the world. At that time, most astronomers believed that the Milky Way was the only galaxy in the universe. During the period from 1922 to 1923, Edwin Hubble made observations with the Hooker Telescope and concluded that the faint smears of light people saw in the night sky were not clouds of gas, as astronomers had thought, but entire galaxies. Furthermore, Hubble proved that these galaxies were moving away, or *receding,* from one another. He also proved that the farther away galaxies were, the faster they were moving. In other words, Hubble showed that the universe is expanding at an astonishing rate.

Picture a deflated balloon with dots drawn so closely together they look like a single dot. Now fill the balloon with air and watch as the dots move away from one another. As with the dots on the inflated balloon, galaxies move away from one another. Of course, a balloon is finite—it has limits. Eventually, it will pop. The universe, on the other hand, could expand forever. Hubble's discovery is now called Hubble's law, and it ranks with other great discoveries, such as Newton's laws of motion and Einstein's theory of relativity. Edwin Hubble developed an equation that uses the speed of light to help calculate just how fast the universe is expanding. The measure of the rate of this expansion is called the Hubble Constant.

If the universe is expanding, then it follows that things must have been compacted at one time. In 1946, Roman Catholic priest, physicist, and astronomer Georges Lemaître (1894–1966), from Belgium, developed the Primeval Atom Hypothesis, the basis for the Big Bang theory, which says everything in the universe that ever was or will be—all matter and all energy—was compressed into a tiny point called a "singularity" or the "cosmic egg." According to Lemaître's hypothesis, which later became a theory, the cosmic egg was about the size of a grain of sand! It was hot and incredibly dense, because it contained all the building blocks of the universe. At some point this packed particle erupted in a fiery burst that created space and everything in it—our universe. This burst is called the Big Bang, the point at which the laws of physics began to apply to the universe.

The term Big Bang is a little misleading because it implies an explosion. A bomb explodes. When it does, matter from the bomb flies off into space that already exists. However, at the moment of the Big Bang, there was no space for anything to explode into. Space and everything else was still contained within the cosmic egg. At that moment, the cosmic egg did not explode *into* space; it erupted, *creating* space that continues to expand. Time as we understand it did not exist before the Big Bang, so scientists cannot explain what went on before it occurred. They can describe only what happened immediately following it in the first ten-millionth of a trillionth of a

Edwin Hubble observing the night sky in 1922, time during which he made his famous discovery about the universe expanding.

LIGHT AND SPEED

Scientists use a figure known as a *light-year* to help them measure the vast distances in our universe. A light-year is the distance light, moving in a vacuum, travels in one year—about 5.9 trillion miles or 186,000 miles per second! Using this figure, we know that light leaving our Sun reaches Earth in 8.3 minutes.

Georges Lemaître in 1933. At the time, he was considered one of the most famous scientists in the world, second only to Albert Einstein.

BETTMANN/CORBIS

trillionth of a second! That unit of measurement is known as Planck time and is represented as 10-43. Named after Max Planck (1858–1947), the German physicist who calculated the measurement, 1 Planck time is the earliest possible instant after the Big Bang that can be determined, and it is when our understanding of the universe begins.

According to the Big Bang theory, the universe quickly expanded from 1 Planck time. And was it hot—ten trillion, trillion times hotter than the core of the Sun! At first the universe was nothing but radiation—energy that is often called the primordial fireball. This fireball was full of the tiniest subatomic particles, called quarks, which in turn formed the earliest atoms. The newborn universe swelled up, and began to cool down. Within three minutes, hydrogen and helium—the most abundant elements in the universe—had formed. During the next million years, gravity pulled the hydrogen and helium into strands called filaments. Around three hundred million years after 1 Planck time, those filaments clumped into clouds of hydrogen and helium and other elements resulting from the Big Bang. Then those clouds came together and formed galaxies, stars, and finally, the planets.

Scientists have been able to explain what happened after the Big Bang, but what happened *before* has remained a nagging question. At this point, most scientists say we simply cannot know. However, remember Mrs. Murry's advice to Meg in *A Wrinkle in Time:* just because something doesn't have an explanation, doesn't mean there isn't one.

For centuries, the age of the universe remained unknown. People could speculate and calculate, but their results were

The Hubble's close-up of some of the oldest galaxies in the universe. They were there long before Earth existed. NASA/ESA/S. Beckwith (STScI) and the HUDF Team

uncertain. The Hubble Space Telescope changed all that. In 1999, Wendy Freedman, an astronomer with the Carnegie Institution for Science, said, "Before Hubble, astronomers could not decide if the universe was ten billion or twenty billion years old." Now that astronomers know the age of the universe, they are able to learn much more about how it began and, perhaps, how it will end. Freedman added, "After all these years, we are finally entering a period of precision cosmology. Now we can more reliably address the broader picture of the universe's origin, evolution, and destiny."

So when did the Big Bang occur? How can science determine the age of the universe? The answers lie in the universe's expansion

THE BIG BOUNCE?

Scientists are always coming up with new hypotheses. In 2007, Martin Bojowald, a physicist working at Pennsylvania State University, proposed an idea explaining what could have happened before the Big Bang. According to Bojowald's hypothesis, our universe may not expand forever. Eventually it could begin contracting, pulling everything in it back into another singularity. That singularity could result in another Big Bang, and a new universe would be born. Furthermore, according to Bojowald, the singularity that became our universe could have been the contraction of a universe that existed before ours. In fact, he suggests the possibility that there could be generations of universes that preceded ours, and generations that will follow, each one bouncing off the singularity that preceded it! Though the theory of the Big Bounce is fascinating, it has not been widely accepted in the scientific community, at least not yet.

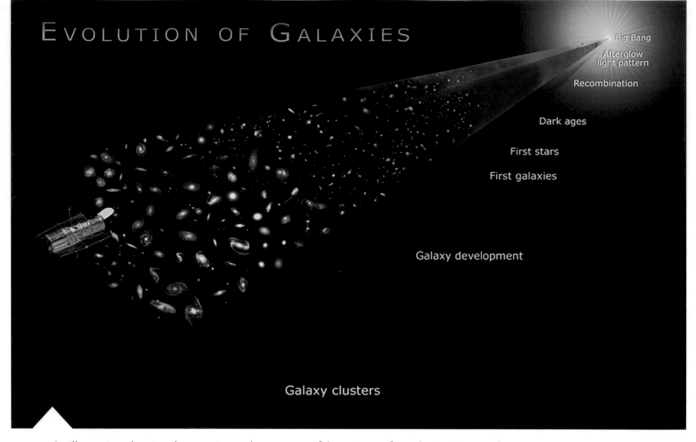

EVOLUTION OF GALAXIES

Big Bang

Afterglow
light pattern

Recombination

Dark ages

First stars

First galaxies

Galaxy development

Galaxy clusters

An illustration showing the cosmic epochs, or ages, of the universe from the Big Bang to the present.
NASA, ESA, AND A. FIELD (STScI)

rate—how fast the galaxies are moving away from one another. We know the faster something goes, the quicker it gets to its destination. Think of a car. If it travels at 60 mph, it will reach its destination faster than if it travels at 30 mph. Speed and time are connected. So if the universe is expanding rapidly, then the galaxies that are farthest away from us would have gotten to where they are quicker than they would have if the universe were expanding slowly. A rapid expansion rate for the universe would indicate that those faraway galaxies are younger than previously thought, because it took them less time to get there.

The Hubble Space Telescope has allowed astronomers to determine that a galaxy appears to gain speed and move away at a rate of 50 miles per second for every 3.2 light-years it is away from Earth. The farther away from Earth it is, the faster it moves—just as Edwin Hubble determined. By using these calculations, and observing the galaxies that are farthest away from us, astronomers now believe our universe is around 13.7 billion years old. If the age of the universe were compared with one 24-hour day, Earth would not have formed until the late afternoon, and humans would have existed for only a few seconds.

EVIDENCE OF THE BIG BANG

Astronomers believe the primordial fireball that immediately followed the Big Bang left a glowing remnant that filled the universe. This telltale glow is called "cosmic microwave background radiation" or CMBR. According to the Big Bang theory, this radiation should be everywhere in the universe. Scientists Arno Penzias and Robert Wilson, working with radio receivers at the Bell Telephone Laboratories in Murray Hill, New Jersey, discovered the existence of cosmic microwave background radiation in 1964. The men heard an annoying hiss in their radios and after ruling out interference from all other sources (and cleaning their antennas from an accumulation of pigeon droppings!) and conducting further studies, they determined that the hiss—which is sometimes called static or noise—was not produced by anything on Earth or even in our solar system. This particular noise was evenly distributed throughout the universe. They had stumbled on the cosmic microwave background radiation that was left over from the Big Bang. In 1978, the men received the Nobel Prize in physics for their discovery.

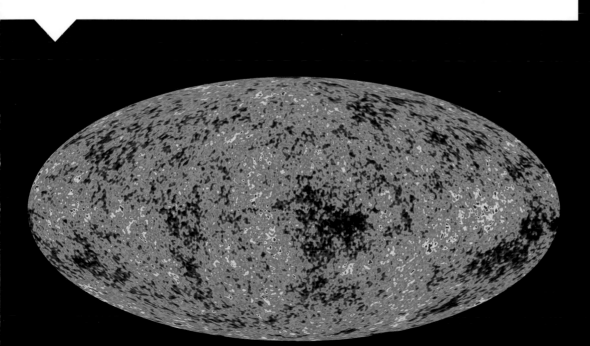

Cosmic microwave background radiation—the oldest light in the universe. This image comes from information collected throughout a period of five years by a space probe called the Wilkinson Microwave Anisotrophy Probe, or WMAP, operated by NASA. NASA/WMAP SCIENCE TEAM

FOUR

THE DARK FORCES AND BLACK HOLES

THERE'S MORE to the universe than meets the eye—about 95 percent more, as a matter of fact. Science has revealed that ordinary matter—the stuff of which galaxies, stars, planets, and people are made—accounts for only 5 percent of what exists. The rest neither produces nor reflects light. Essentially, it's invisible. How do scientists know about it, then? Because these mysterious substances, called dark matter and dark energy, have gravity, and gravity always has an effect on the things that surround it, an effect that can be observed.

Stars and galaxies are in constant motion. The stars in individual galaxies orbit around a galaxy's center. Gravity pulls galaxies together into small groups called clusters. The clusters, in turn, orbit around the center of their collection of galaxies. Furthermore, as the universe expands, the swirling clusters of galaxies, like the dots on an inflating balloon, move away from one another as space stretches between them.

The Hubble captures a ghostly ring of dark matter in a cluster of galaxies. This picture, created by Hubble scientists, is a combination of two images. The dark ring is an astronomical map that has been layered on top of the image of the galaxy cluster. The map shows astronomers how the cluster's gravity is distorting the light that is coming to the telescope from more distant galaxies. Discovered in May 2007, this ring is one of the strongest pieces of evidence to date for the existence of the dark matter that scientists believe makes up most of the universe's material.
NASA/ESA, M. J. JEE, AND H. FORD (JOHNS HOPKINS UNIVERSITY)

Fritz Zwicky, working at the California Institute of Technology. He is credited with the discovery of the force that came to be known as dark matter.
AIP Emilio Sergre Visual Archives

Dr. Adam Riess, leader of a team of astronomers who discovered dark energy in 1998. W. Kirk, Homewood Photographic Services, Johns Hopkins University

In the 1930s a Swiss astronomer named Fritz Zwicky (1898–1974) noticed strange behavior in a cluster of galaxies he was studying. Some of the galaxies were whirling around the center of their cluster in an orbit that was so fast, they should have been flung out into the universe, away from their home cluster. Instead, they remained in their group. Something very powerful at the center of the cluster was keeping the racing galaxies in orbit. Zwicky determined that whatever it was had to be massive and have a lot of gravity—more gravity than all the galaxies in the cluster put together. Although he couldn't see it, he knew there was something keeping the galaxies in place, just as one knows the wind—which is not visible—is present when a flag flutters in the breeze. The mysterious substance became known as dark matter.

Astronomers now believe that dark matter surrounds all galaxies and extends out into the universe. Of course, no one knows what dark matter is made of, because no one has ever been able to detect a single particle in it. Still, scientists believe dark matter accounts for about 23 percent of the universe's makeup.

Because of dark matter and its gravitational pull, cosmologists hypothesized that the universe would eventually stop expanding, and might even begin contracting, which could result in something like a Big Crunch—the opposite of the Big Bang—billions of years from now. But they were in for a surprise.

In 1998, Dr. Adam Riess (born 1969), an astrophysicist working at the Space Telescope Science Institute and at Johns Hopkins University, was part of a team that used ground-based telescopes and the Hubble Space Telescope to study the expansion of the universe. "Our aim was to use supernovae—a special kind of exploding star—to measure how fast the universe was expanding in the past and then to compare it with how fast it is expanding now," he said. The team wanted to see if gravity from dark matter was causing the universe to put on the brakes, so to speak, and they wanted to know by how much the expansion was slowing down. They made an unexpected—and astonishing—discovery: The universe is actually speeding up! Dr. Riess said, "If you tossed a ball into the air and it kept right on going up, instead of falling to the ground, you would undoubtedly be very surprised. Well, that's about how surprised we were with this result." The same result was obtained independently by another team of astronomers led by Dr. Saul Perlmutter of the Lawrence Berkeley National Laboratories. Although the pull of dark matter was holding clusters of galaxies together in a group, another invisible force was pushing these cluster groups apart—and pushing them apart fast! This force has been named dark energy, and it remains one of the most studied, yet least understood, forces in the universe.

Research into dark energy and dark matter is just getting under way. The Hubble Space Telescope, along with other observatories, will help scientists look for explanations for these dark mysteries in the universe.

There is another kind of darkness in the universe that has captured imaginations around the world, and become part of our everyday language. When a toy, tool, or other object disappears and cannot be found, often it is said it has fallen into a black hole, meaning it has inexplicably and irretrievably disappeared. Of course, there are no black holes on Earth, and most likely the object in question is findable. But there are black holes in space, and anything that

GRAVITY: HOLDING THINGS TOGETHER

Gravity is the force in the universe that makes all objects pull on, or attract, one another. Objects can be visible matter, such as stars and planets, or they can be invisible, such as dark matter. Scientists now know that visible and invisible matter exert gravity. The more mass, or substance, an object (matter) has, the more gravity it has. On Earth, we know that what goes up, always must come down. Fruit falls from a tree, a baby bird falls from a nest, and a person falls off a bike because Earth is more massive than fruit, a bird, or a person. Earth's gravity pulls everything on Earth toward itself—and gravity is what keeps you from falling off Earth and out into space. Gravity exists throughout the universe.

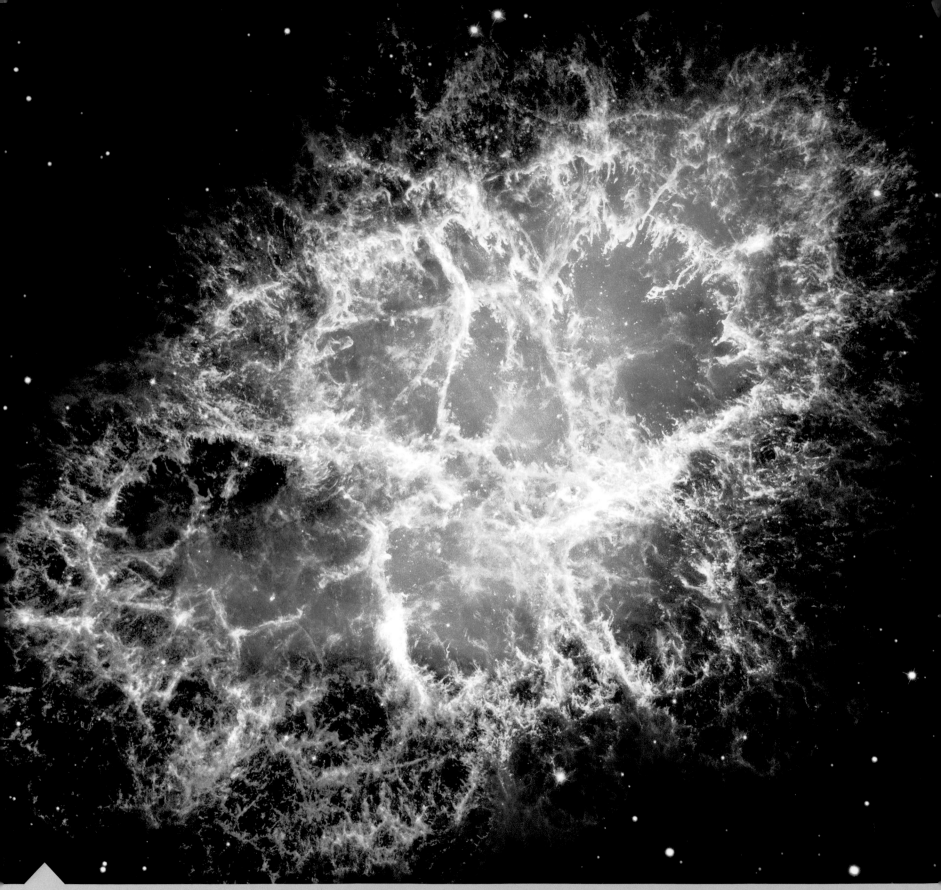

A supernova explosion in the Crab Nebula. The orange filaments are the remains of the star and are mostly hydrogen. In 1054, Japanese and Chinese astronomers recorded this event. The Hubble Space Telescope photographed it in 2005. NASA, ESA, J. HESTER, AND A. LOLL (ARIZONA STATE UNIVERSITY)

disappears into one *is* gone forever. There is no escape from an astronomical black hole, because the pull of its gravity is too strong.

Escaping the force of gravity isn't easy, and the more massive an object is, the harder it is to escape its gravitational pull. For example, during each *Apollo* Moon mission, the rockets carrying the astronauts had to reach 25,000 mph, known as Earth's *escape velocity,* to escape Earth's gravity. When the astronauts left the Moon to return home, their spacecraft had to reach a speed of only 5,300 mph to escape the Moon's gravitational pull. Why? Because the Moon is smaller than Earth and has less mass. Escape velocities are determined by the ratio of an object's mass to its radius—the imaginary line that goes from the center of a sphere to its perimeter. Different objects in the universe have different escape velocities. Nothing in the entire universe is more compact (having a higher ratio of mass to radius) or more compressed than a black hole.

American physicist John Wheeler (1911–2008) gave black holes their name in 1967 in a speech he delivered at the Goddard Institute of Space Studies. It's a clever name, but of course a black hole isn't really a hole. One simplified definition of a black hole is that it's an object whose escape velocity is equal to or exceeds the speed of light. Nothing can go faster than the speed of light; therefore, nothing can escape from a black hole.

One type of black hole forms when the core of a massive star—twenty or more times the size of our Sun—stops fusing light atoms into heavier ones. That fusion process creates nuclear energy, which heats up the gases and makes the star shine. As the dying star, called a supernova, runs out of its nuclear fuel, it explodes in

ORBITS: STAYING CLOSE TO HOME

When the space shuttle *Atlantis* left Earth and carried the astronauts to the Hubble Space Telescope, it was traveling at about 17,500 mph. At that speed, Earth's gravity was still in effect. *Atlantis* did not continue to zoom past the Hubble and out into space. Instead, Earth's gravity pulled the shuttle downward and into a circle that matched the curvature of Earth. After a series of maneuvers, the shuttle moved into the same orbit as the Hubble Space Telescope, and both literally fell into orbit around Earth.

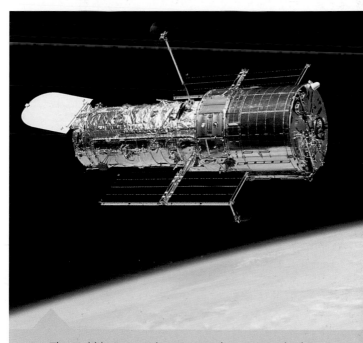

The Hubble Space Telescope travels in a curved orbit around Earth and will not hurtle off into space. Here the Hubble casts a ghostly reflection off the shuttle's window. NASA/ESA

John Wheeler in 1973. Note the imaginative drawing of a black hole in the background.
AIP EMILIO SEGRE VISUAL ARCHIVES, WHEELER COLLECTION

a tremendous burst of light and energy, throwing its outer layers into the universe. If less than three times the mass of the star remains in the core after the layers are shed, then the supernova will become a neutron star. Alternatively, if *more* than three times the mass of the star remains after the shedding, the core will keep on collapsing until what is left of the star's mass is packed into one tiny dense point, called, like the cosmic egg that formed the universe, a singularity. Of course, a star's singularity is not the same as the cosmic egg. It contains all the condensed matter from the core of the star, not the entire universe. But the gravity exerted by this super-dense object is strong enough to warp the spacetime that surrounds it.

This warped, bent area around a black hole is called the *event horizon*. Anything that crosses the event horizon—stars, gas, dust,

This artist's image shows a star that has survived the supernova explosion that created a black hole, but its survival will be short-lived. As the star orbits the black hole some of its matter crosses the event horizon and is sucked into it. Right before it disappears, the star's matter emits jets of gas that stream away from the black hole system at 90 percent the speed of light.
ESA/NASA AND FELIX MIRABEL (FRENCH ATOMIC ENERGY COMMISSION AND INSTITUTE FOR ASTRONOMY AND SPACE PHYSICS/CONICET OF ARGENTINA)

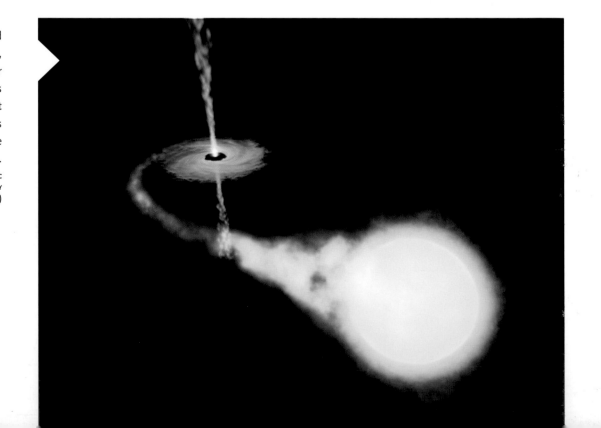

asteroids, and even light—will be drawn into the black hole. In space, anything that comes to the edge of the event horizon will be pulled into the black hole.

Though they weren't called black holes back then, these mysterious areas of space were first noted in the 1790s, when two scientists, John Michell (1724–1793) of England and Pierre-Simon, marquis de Laplace (1749–1827) of France, were studying Newton's laws of motion. Working separately, each man came up with a hypothesis about a possible invisible star in the universe. The hypothesis became a theory, but for centuries no one could find evidence of the existence of these invisible stars, or black holes. The Hubble Space Telescope cannot see black holes, either, but it has photographed the activity that surrounds some of them, evidence that strongly supports their existence.

BENDING SPACETIME

The theory of relativity states, among other things, that spacetime can actually be shaped, or bent, by mass. Picture the surface of a trampoline and think of it as spacetime. If you stand on its surface, your body and its mass will make the trampoline's surface bend inward around your feet. Now imagine someone placing a tennis ball on the edge of the indentation your body has made in the trampoline's surface. That ball will roll inward, toward your feet. It has to happen. But if someone places a tennis ball outside the curve made with your body's mass, the ball will stay put. A black hole's mass works similarly in space, bending it inward to infinity.

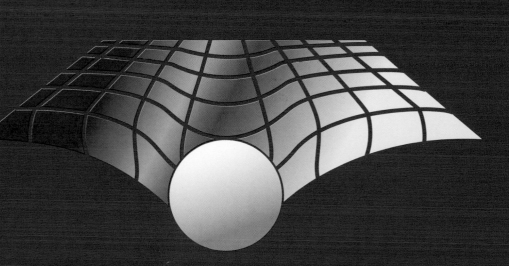

An illustration showing the effect the mass of our Sun has on the surrounding spacetime. Think of spacetime as fabric, capable of being stretched and even torn. Note how the curve of spacetime is steeper near the Sun, and weaker farther away. Note, too, how spacetime is stretched nearer the Sun. All spacetime curves and stretches more when it is close to a mass, and time is slightly different closer to the Sun, though not so much that you would notice it. If the mass is very large, then the dent in spacetime will be very deep. In fact, it can be so deep that the heavy object breaks through spacetime—tears it—and forms a black hole. Nothing escapes from a black hole, and science cannot say what is on the other side.

The Hubble captured this bluish stream of electrons and other subatomic particles being ejected from a massive black hole at the center of Galaxy M87. The yellow glow is billions of stars, too far away for the Hubble to see individually. Astronomers calculate that the black hole has consumed enough of these stars and the gas that surrounds them to equal to two *billion* stars the size of our Sun! NASA AND THE HUBBLE HERITAGE TEAM (STScI/AURA)

An artist's depiction of a star in the process of being destroyed by a black hole. The black hole is pulling on the front of the star more strongly than on the back, stretching the star out and causing its gases to fall into the black hole. M. WEISS, CXC, NASA

One monstrous black hole resides in Messier 87 or M87, an enormous galaxy located fifty million miles away from Earth. Astronomers estimate that it could weigh as much as three *billion* times the mass of our Sun! It was discovered when the Hubble detected a rapid increase in starlight at the center of M87. Astronomers studied the motion of gas at the galaxy's center and concluded that gravity from a massive black hole must be pulling the stars near it inward. As the stars fall into a black hole, they shed their layers of gas, causing brightness. The escaping gas heats up to millions of degrees Fahrenheit and travels at about 99 percent of the speed of light. As it cools, it forms into bubbles approximately 200,000 light-years across, or about twice the diameter of our Milky Way galaxy.

So far, astronomers have detected at least thirteen black holes that are busily gobbling up matter in the Milky Way. However, the closest of these entities is still a whopping 3,000 to 4,000 light-years from Earth. That's far enough away that there's no danger Earth will ever cross any of their event horizons.

FIVE

THE LIFE CYCLE OF A STAR

IF YOU HAVE good eyesight and live in an area where the view of the night sky is not polluted with city lights, you might be able to see, very roughly, about two thousand stars in the sky—though that number may vary. Since Earth is divided into two hemispheres—north and south—your neighbors living in the opposite hemisphere might also be able to see about two thousand stars. So a total of four thousand stars—more or less—are visible from the surface of Earth. However, that is only a tiny percentage of the 100 billion stars in our Milky Way galaxy alone. Multiply that number by at least another 100 billion, and you may come close to the number of stars in the universe. Most of the light in the universe is produced by stars.

Stars have a life cycle—stages of development—just as living things do. Stars are born, they grow to maturity—a period called their *main sequence*—and become old and die. The entire sequence can take millions of years and often much longer.

Thousands of stars are forming within the clouds of rolling gas and dust in this portion of the Orion Nebula. NASA, ESA, AND A. FIELD (STScI)

All stars begin their lives in a cloud of space gas—made mostly of hydrogen mixed with grains of space dust—that is called a *nebula*. A nebula is a cloud of gas and dust that glows—usually due to light from nearby stars. Often called "star factories," nebulae are classified according to whether they emit, absorb, or reflect light. Within the nebula, gravity pulls the hydrogen atoms together into a globule of gas that starts to spin. Eventually the spinning creates a central core within the globule of gas, which is heated up by contraction. This heated core is surrounded by a flat, pancake-like disk of leftover dust. When the core's heat reaches about eighteen *million* degrees Fahrenheit, the hydrogen fuses into helium, in a process called nuclear fusion. The star comes to life and begins to glow because of the radiation from the nuclear energy.

It can take anywhere from ten thousand to one million years before nuclear fusion takes place and a star is ready to shine. Once a star reaches this stage, called its main sequence, it continues to convert its supply of hydrogen into helium, depending on its size, for millions—or billions—of years. On Earth, countries have used nuclear fusion to create weapons, but the capacity of explosion of these weapons, tremendous though it may be, is nothing compared with the nuclear fusion inside a star.

When living things die on Earth, they decompose. As they decompose their elements return to the earth, enriching the environment—the soil, the air, the ocean—so new life can begin and established life can continue thriving. So it is with stars. As they die they release material into the cosmos, providing the building blocks for future generations of stars, planets, and perhaps life itself. The atoms that make up our Sun and its solar system, and

The Hubble's instruments captured these stars, packed together in a cluster called NGC 6397. They are located 8,200 light-years away from Earth. The bright blue stars near the center of the cluster are young stars, burning hot and bright. NASA AND THE HUBBLE HERITAGE TEAM (AURA/STScI)

TYPES OF STARS

A star's lifetime is determined by its mass, and a star's mass is determined by the amount of space dust and gas in the nebula in which the star formed. The larger a star is, the shorter its life will be. There are five levels of star formation: very low-mass stars, low-mass stars, intermediate-mass stars, high-mass stars, and very high-mass stars.

▶ **VERY LOW-MASS STARS:** A very low-mass star is called a brown dwarf. Brown dwarfs are stars that fizzled out early in their development. They simply do not have enough mass to fuse hydrogen into helium as a true star does, though they can give off some light and heat. Brown dwarfs are known as substellar objects. In other words, they are not quite stars, but they're close. Brown dwarfs can live for approximately 100 trillion years.

▶ **LOW-MASS STARS:** A low-mass star is a true star, because it produces nuclear fusion. Sometimes called red dwarfs, low-mass stars tend to keep their size all their lives, roughly a trillion years. At the end of its life cycle, it is known as a white dwarf.

▶ **INTERMEDIATE-MASS STARS:** Like all true stars, an intermediate-mass star fuses hydrogen into helium. After it has lived out its mature lifetime, an intermediate-mass star begins to change. As its supply of

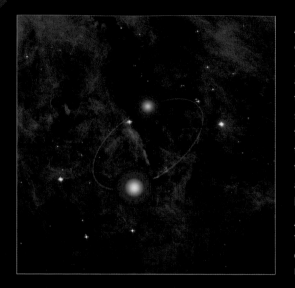

An artist's image of two actual brown dwarfs, mysterious celestial objects that astronomers theorize start out as big as a star, but somehow shrink and cool as they age and end up being closer to the size of a planet. One of these dwarfs is fifty-five times more massive than Jupiter; the other is thirty-five times bigger. In order to burn hydrogen through nuclear fusion and qualify as true stars, the dwarfs would have to be eighty times more massive than Jupiter. An analysis of the light coming from these brown dwarfs showed that the dwarfs had a reddish cast.
NASA/ESA AND A. FELID (STScI)

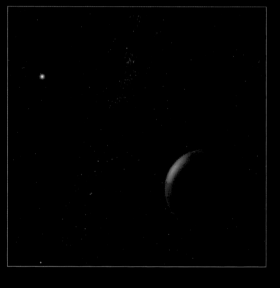

An artist's concept of red dwarf star CHRX 73 (upper left) and its companion object, CHRX 73 b. Astronomers say the companion object is small enough to be a planet, but also large enough to be a brown dwarf; therefore, they have not decided whether CHRX 73 b is a planet or not. The young star is two million years old and only five hundred light-years away from Earth.
NASA/ESA AND G. BACON (STScI)

The Hubble's cameras took this picture of the remains of a supernova that exploded 160,000 light-years from our own Milky Way galaxy. It is estimated that the star that produced this enormous explosion was fifty times more massive than our Sun. A few million years from now, this gas and dust may be part of the formation of new stars and new planets.
NASA, ESA, HEIC, AND THE HUBBLE HERITAGE TEAM (STScI/AURA)

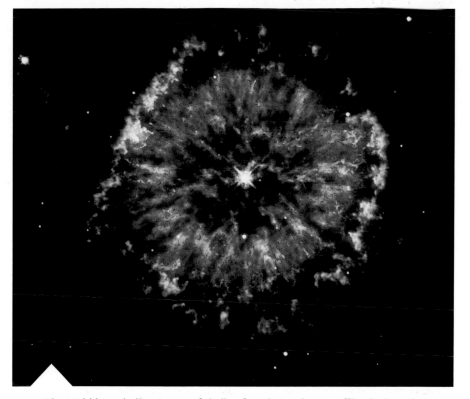

The Hubble took this picture of shells of gas being thrown off by the hot white star at the center of the nebula. Our star, the Sun, is predicted to eject its own planetary nebula around six billion years from now. **NASA/THE HUBBLE HERITAGE TEAM (STScI/AURA)**

the atoms that make up our own bodies, were once part of a star. In this way, Earth and its people, plants, animals—everything—are literally made of stardust.

Our closest star is the Sun, located 93 million miles away from Earth. Although the Hubble's instruments cannot photograph our own Sun or the planet Mercury (because it is too close to the Sun), they have provided hundreds of amazing images of star birth and death throughout the universe. Two of the new instruments installed on the Hubble during the 2009 mission—the Cosmic Origins Spectrograph and the Wide Field Camera 3—will allow astronomers and other scientists to study the stars with great clarity for years to come.

Continued from page 42.

hydrogen is depleted, it literally runs out of gas. A sudden burst of energy at its core then causes the star to expand and swell, as its outer layers are expelled into the universe as a planetary nebula. The swollen star is now called a red giant. Eventually, the core of a red giant star will contract into a white dwarf. Our Sun is an intermediate-mass star. Astronomers believe the Sun is 4.6 billion years old, and will live for ten billion years, the average life span for this kind of star. Eventually, the Sun will become a red giant.

▶ **VERY HIGH-MASS STARS:** A very high-mass star fuses hydrogen into helium at an extremely fast rate. These huge stars—about a hundred times larger than our Sun—have a relatively short main sequence life of about a million years. As a very high-mass star moves out of its main sequence and the core collapses, the star material that surrounds it is sent flying into space in an explosion called a supernova. A supernova releases more energy in ten seconds than our Sun will produce during its entire ten-billion-year lifetime. The core that remains either becomes a neutron star—the tiniest star of all—or it continues collapsing until it becomes a black hole.

SIX

RECIPE FOR A PLANET

INGREDIENTS

You will need:

1 intermediate-mass star

1 nebula containing leftover stardust

millions of pounds gravitational pressure

millions of years' time

Instructions

Using gravitational pressure, whirl nebula containing stardust around the star. Watch until it forms into a flattened, pancake-like disk. Disk will not be uniform or smooth. It will contain large and small clumps of matter. Allow gravity to continue whirling disk around star. Check to see if larger clumps in disk are colliding with smaller clumps. Large clumps should be migrating inward, toward the star, leaving smaller clumps on the

An artist's depiction of the formation of a solar system similar to Earth's. Note the ring of dusty debris— all that remains from the original protoplanetary disk that orbited the star. Closer to the star are orbiting planets.
NASA/JPL-Caltech/T. Pyle/SSC

outer edges. This is normal. Allow process to continue for millions of years. Check disk. Smaller clumps may have disappeared from disk, or become comets, asteroids, and other space debris. Remaining large clumps of matter should now be whirling around central star, each in its own orbit. If so, planets are done.

Yield: Varies, depending on amount of matter in your original nebula. On Earth, the yield is eight planets. Your batch could be larger, or smaller.

Caution: Most planets will be uninhabitable.

Although this recipe is fanciful, it does explain the bare bones of planetary formation. Planets are made from leftovers—the materials remaining after a star has formed. Stars are born in the bits of gas and space dust, or nebulae, that are rotating around them, but not all the material goes into the star's core. After a star begins to shine, the remaining dust, gas, and ice continue swirling around the star and form a flat disk called a *protoplanetary disk*.

Gravity is at work in the protoplanetary disk, just as it is at work in the star. As the disk rotates around the star, gravity causes the particles of dust, ice, and gas to begin sticking together in clumps called *planetesimals*. The bigger the planetesimals get, the more gravity they have. Larger planetesimals attract smaller ones and if they merge, they create objects called *protoplanets*. The protoplanets continue to grow as gravity pulls at their cores, shaping them into spheres, ball-like objects. Sometimes these spheres crash into one another like celestial billiard balls. That kind of action sends smaller objects out of the path of the larger ones and to the outer reaches

The Hubble's cameras took this image of clouds of dust and gas in a small section of the Orion nebula, a region of space that is churning out new stars. The gas is illuminated and heated by ultraviolet light from four hot, massive stars in the nebula. NASA, C. R. O'DELL, AND S. K. WONG (RICE UNIVERSITY)

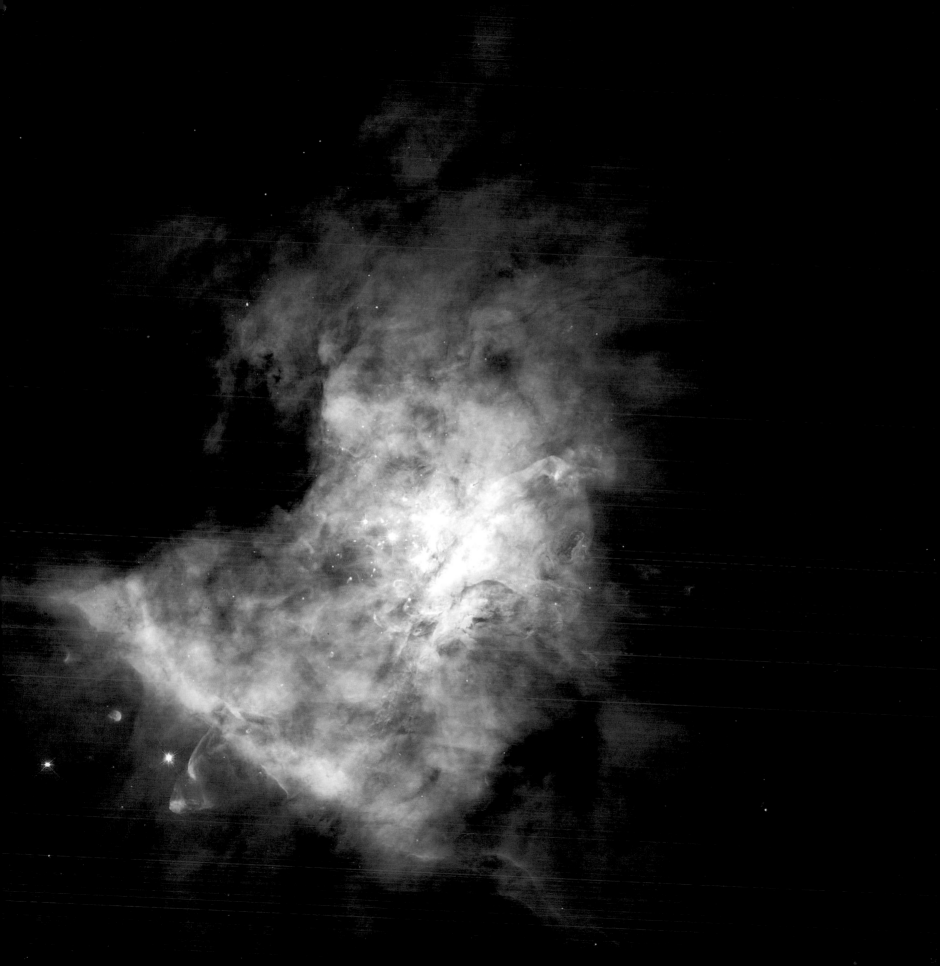

WHAT IS A PLANET?

The International Astronomical Union is the official body that identifies and names planets. Surprisingly, there had been no official scientific definition for a planet until the IAU decided on one on August 24, 2006. The following definition excludes Pluto from consideration. The IAU defines a planet as a celestial body that

▶ orbits the Sun

▶ is round or almost round

▶ has enough gravity to clear the area around its orbit

of the solar system, where they become dwarf planets, asteroids, and comets. The remaining large spheres become the planets traveling alone in their orbits around their host star.

For centuries, scientists believed our solar system—Earth and its eight planets—to be the only one in the universe. Although astronomers and other scientists had speculated about the existence of other planets, in the 1990s telescopes from the ground and the Hubble Space Telescope aided astronomers in making the first discoveries of other planets orbiting other stars outside our solar system. Those planets are called *exoplanets*.

Even before the Hubble was launched, in the 1980s, some astronomers hypothesized that a star in the southern constellation of Pices Australis, or the Southern Fish, might have a planet or two in its orbit. The star's name was Fomalhaut, which means "whale's mouth" in Arabic, and it is the brightest star in its constellation. In 2004, an instrument onboard the Hubble called the Advanced Camera for Surveys (ACS) detected an enormous protoplanetary

In 2006, the Hubble Space Telescope's instruments detected the presence of this Jupiter-sized planet orbiting a young (eight hundred million years!) star in our galaxy. At 10.5 light-years away, it is the closest planet outside those of our solar system. This is an artist's concept of what the planet looks like, since its star is still surrounded by a disk of dust that extends into space twenty billion miles. Hubble could only detect the planet's presence by measuring the gravitational pull, or tug, it had on its star.
NASA/ESA AND G. BACON (STScI)

disk, 21.5 *billion* miles across, in orbit around Fomalhaut. In 2005, the Hubble's cameras were able to capture an actual image of the protoplanetary disk.

Paul Kalas, an astronomer working at the University of California, Berkeley, along with a team of other astronomers, suggested that gravity—and therefore a mass—was tugging on the disk. Scientists wondered whether the gravity of a planet was pulling on it. Finally, in November 2008, they discovered that there was a planet orbiting Fomalhaut. The Hubble's cameras photographed it. The planet, which is three times the size of Jupiter, was named Fomalhaut b.

It takes time and patience to be a scientific planet hunter. Paul Kalas said, "Our Hubble observations were incredibly demanding. Fomalhaut b is one billion times fainter than the star. We began this program in 2001 and our persistence has finally paid off." His team member Mark Clampin of NASA's Goddard Space Flight Center added, "The lesson for exoplanet hunters is 'follow the dust.'"

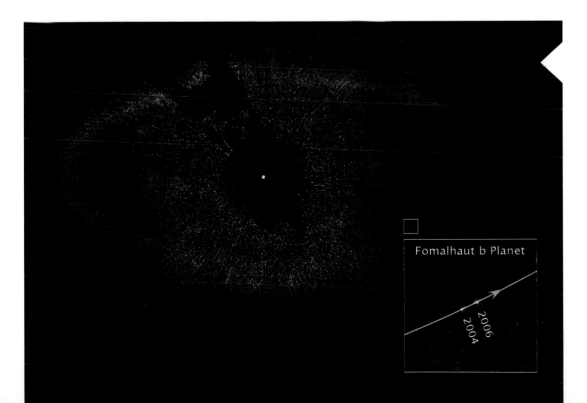

The Hubble captured the star Fomalhaut surrounded by its protoplanetary disk. Inside the disk to the right, the planet Fomalhaut b has formed and is in orbit. Astronomers use movement to detect the presence of exoplanets. Note the movement of Fomalhaut b from 2004 to 2006. NASA, ESA, AND P. KALAS (UNIVERSITY OF CALIFORNIA, BERKELEY)

Although Fomalhaut is an intermediate-mass star, it is much larger than our Sun—and much brighter, too. In fact, Fomalhaut, which is located in the southern hemisphere, is the seventeenth brightest star in the night sky. Fomalhaut is a very young star—about one hundred to three hundred million years old. It is burning its hydrogen so fast that astronomers think it will burn out in about one billion years. That's a short life span for a star, mostly likely not enough time to give life any chance to develop on Fomalhaut b.

That does not mean some form of life could not exist on one of the many hundred other exoplanets that have been discovered with the help of the Hubble since 1995. Like Fomalhaut b, most have been large Jupiter-like gas giants, not rocky terrestrial planets like Earth. To support life, a planet would have to have the right conditions to store carbon, oxygen, hydrogen, and nitrogen, the chemical building blocks necessary for life, as we know it, to exist. The planet would also have to have a source of liquid water, and be the right distance from its star so it would be neither too hot nor too cold. It would need the right atmosphere of gases to support life, too. In other words, it would have to be pretty similar to Earth.

So far, out of the hundreds of billions of stars in the universe, no one has found another Earth. But that doesn't mean one doesn't exist, or that, aided by the Hubble, scientists won't be able to find it.

As the characters in *A Wrinkle in Time* discovered, our universe is a wondrous place. And while it is mysterious to be sure, solving its mysteries is now within the realm of possibility.

The Hubble's instruments searched this field of stars, looking for planets. The telescope found nine stars (circled in green) that have planets orbiting them. Astronomers can detect the presence of a planet by observing the gravity it exerts on its star as it orbits. Gravity tugs on the star, causing it to wobble. Astronomers can also detect a planet in orbit when it eclipses, or passes in front of, its star, partially blocking out its light. Astronomical instruments can measure the frequency of the eclipses, and determine if an object like a planet is in orbit around the star. Only time will tell if another Earth-like planet is out there somewhere. THE HUBBLE HERITAGE TEAM (AURA/STScI/NASA)

As humans, we will continue to study the cosmos and wonder: Where did we come from? What is our fate? Are there others out there, asking the same questions we ask? As science moves forward, each generation will ask more questions and make more discoveries than the generation preceding it. The body of knowledge will grow as we seek scientific answers to the question of *how* the universe came to be the way it is.

Why the universe exists is an entirely different question—one that science cannot answer. We each must answer that question for ourselves.

AFTERWORD

AFTER 12 days, 21 hours, and 37 minutes in space, the crew of STS-125 finally returned to Earth, their mission complete. At a welcome home ceremony at the Johnson Space Center, "Hubble Hugger" John Grunsfeld said, "Hubble is an evolving story . . . that story isn't at the end with the termination of our mission. It's really the beginning of a brand new Hubble story. We're looking forward to the great science that will come out of Hubble."

In the afterglow of the successfully completed mission, however, there was a three-month wait before anyone could begin to use the telescope once again. The new instruments onboard the Hubble had to go through a process called outgassing. Despite every effort to keep the Hubble instruments sterile while they were on Earth, there was some contamination—molecules of earthly gas attached themselves to the instruments and traveled into space with them. Because even one molecule of unwanted gas could interfere with the instruments' ability to function, everyone had to

One of the Hubble's first images after the servicing mission shows a gas jet in the Carina Nebula.
NASA, ESA, AND THE HUBBLE SM4 ERO TEAM

53

wait for several weeks while outgassing—allowing the unwanted molecules to simply float away into space—took place.

Additionally, small parts within the instruments were out of alignment. When instruments went from having weight on Earth to being weightless in space, small mirrors inside them moved slightly. Engineers on Earth were able to gently shift the mirrors back into their proper positions via computers connected to the Hubble. This process also took a few weeks.

Finally, the instruments had to be calibrated. When an instrument is calibrated, it is adjusted to match a given norm. For example, if you wanted to make sure a bathroom scale was accurate, you could put a ten-pound weight on it, and check to see if the scale registered exactly ten pounds. If the scale read 10.2 pounds, you would know it needed to be adjusted, or calibrated, to read the correct weight.

Astronomers calibrated the Hubble's instruments by measuring their data, or information, against a known astronomical value. Instead of the ten-pound weight used to calibrate the bathroom scale, the astronomers compared the instruments' readings with past observations they knew were accurate. They carefully adjusted the Hubble's instruments to ensure that any new observations would be absolutely precise and the images completely clear.

At last, in September 2009, the Hubble was ready to show off its new capabilities. The pressroom at NASA headquarters was crowded with reporters eager to see what the Hubble saw. Others all over the world tuned in as well. Ten million hits came into the

These are the first images that were released after the Hubble was repaired. They include a butterfly-shaped nebula (opposite) and a densely packed cluster of stars (p. 56). NASA/ESA AND THE HUBBLE SM4 ERO TEAM

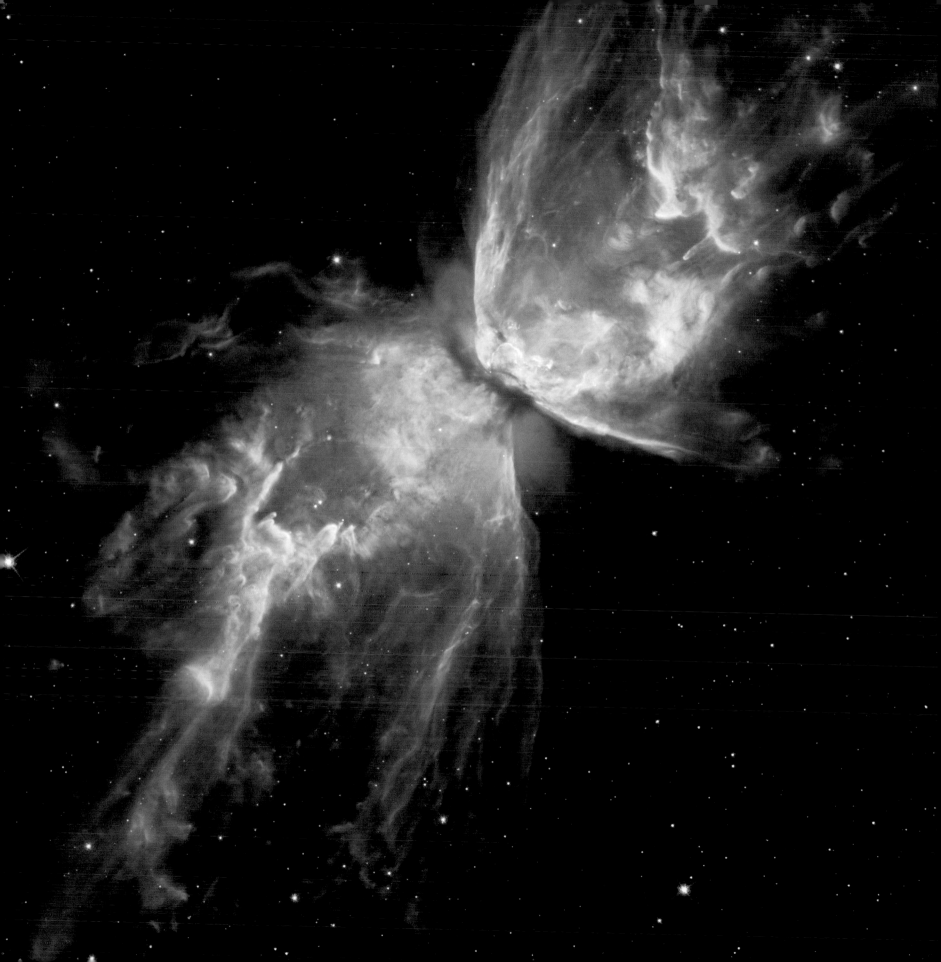

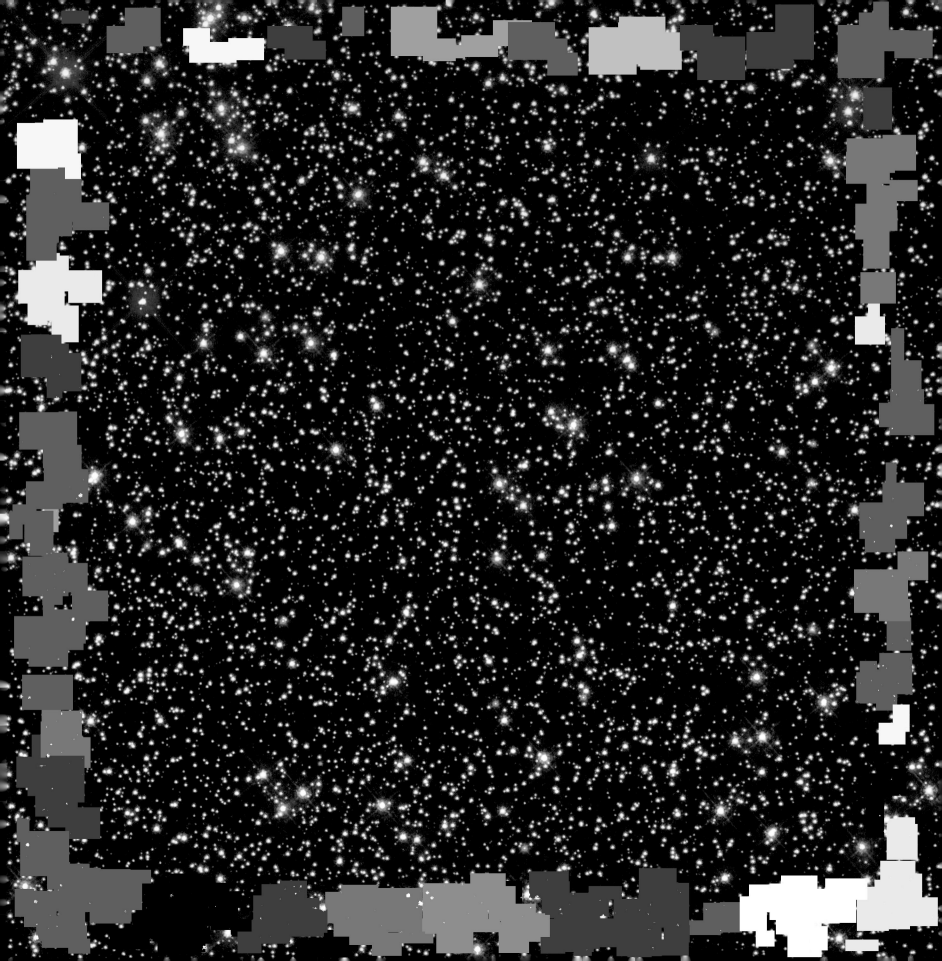

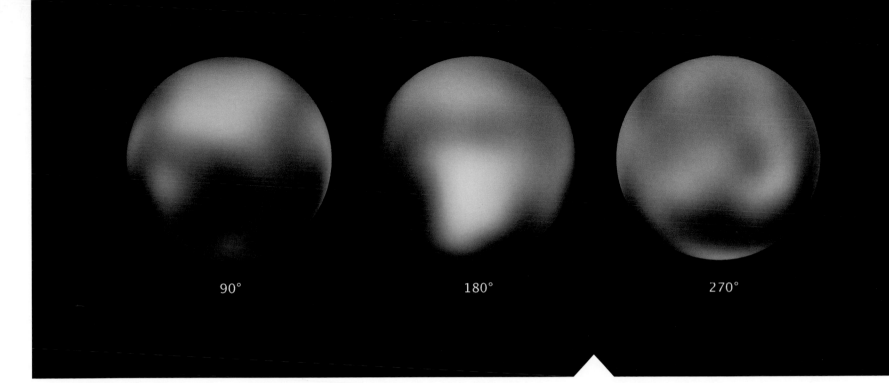

90°   180°   270°

The Hubble's camera took these images of Pluto's surface—the most detailed that have ever been seen of the dwarf planet. The photographs show seasonal changes, as Pluto goes through its 248-year-long orbit of the Sun. **NASA**

computer server at Space Telescope Science Institute, slowing it down for two days. "Not that we minded," said Rachel Osten, an astronomer at the institute. "We all knew the reason why!"

In Washington, D.C., Edward Weiler, associate administrator for NASA's Science Mission Directorate, said, "This marks a new beginning for Hubble. The telescope was given an extreme make-over and now is significantly more powerful than ever, well equipped to last into the next decade." Maryland senator Barbara Mikulski, who had worked to make the Hubble mission happen, said, "I fought for the Hubble repair mission because Hubble is the people's telescope. I also fought for Hubble because it constantly rewrites the science textbooks. It has more discoveries than any other science mission. Hubble is our greatest example of our astronauts working together with scientists to show American leadership and ingenuity."

The upgraded Hubble Space Telescope released this image of hundreds of brilliant blue stars. Several of these stars are one hundred times more massive than our Sun.

NASA/ESA, F. Panesce (NAF-IASF, Bologna, Italy), R. O'Connell (University of Virginia, Charlottesville), and the Wide Field Camera 3 Science Oversight Committee

Astronomers, astronauts, and everyone else who is curious about the universe will continue to follow the Hubble's discoveries until the great observatory comes to the end of its useful life, probably around or just before 2020. No further repair missions are scheduled for it.

Fortunately, another great observatory, the James Webb Space Telescope, is waiting to be launched in 2014. Named after a former administrator of NASA, the James Webb is being constructed to see in the infrared wavelengths in an area of space much farther from Earth than the Hubble can, where there is a constant magnetic field. The James Webb will be used to study four scientific themes: the end of the Dark Ages and First Light in the universe, the assembly of galaxies, the birth of stars and protoplanetary systems, and planetary systems and the origins of life. It will continue the work the Hubble began, casting a probing eye upon the universe, so we can continue to appreciate its beauty and uncover more of its deepest mysteries.

USING THE HUBBLE

Astronomers and others working at the Space Telescope Science Institute (STScI) in Baltimore, Maryland, do a lot of observing with the Hubble, but they also make it available to other astronomers around the world. Each year, the institute receives around one thousand requests, asking permission to use the Hubble. These requests are made in the form of proposals, which say—among other things—what area of the sky astronomers want to observe and the purpose of their observations—what it is they are hoping to discover. The proposals are submitted to STScI and evaluated by an international panel of scientists. There are usually six requests for every proposal granted, so getting an opportunity to use the Hubble is a competitive endeavor! The Hubble works twenty-four hours a day, seven days a week. Because of its heavy workload, on average, more than eight scientific papers per week are published based on its observations. In addition, astronomers and others present their findings at scientific conferences around the world, so everyone benefits from this remarkable scientific instrument. Because of the success of STS-125, astronomers can make their observations with the upgraded Hubble in a fraction of the time that was needed before. Therefore, more observations will be possible well into the future.

- **ASTRONAUT:** A person trained to take part in a space flight.

- **ASTRONOMY:** The study of stars, planets, and other celestial bodies outside Earth's atmosphere.

- **ASTROPHYSICIST:** An astronomer who studies the behavior and physical properties of celestial bodies and phenomena.

- **ATMOSPHERE:** The gases surrounding the surface of a planet, moon, or star.

- **ATOM:** The smallest unit, or part, of any chemical element.

- **BIG BANG THEORY:** A theory that states the universe erupted from a singularity, or cosmic egg.

- **BLACK HOLE:** A celestial object that has a gravitational field so strong, nothing, not even light, can escape.

- **CAPE CANAVERAL:** Launch site in eastern Florida of the United States' space flights.

- **COSMIC BACKGROUND RADIATION:** Radiation that filled the universe after the Big Bang and is still detectable.

- **COSMIC EGG:** The singularity that contained all the matter of the universe before the Big Bang.

- **DARK ENERGY:** A mysterious force that is pushing galaxies apart and thought to be the cause of the accelerating expansion of the universe.

- **DARK MATTER:** A mysterious substance that accounts for 23 percent of the universe. It is not visible or directly detectable but has gravitational pull.

- **ESCAPE VELOCITY:** The speed required to exit the gravitational pull of a planet or moon.

- **EVENT HORIZON:** The area that borders a black hole. Once an object crosses the event horizon, it will be sucked into the black hole.

- **EXOPLANETS:** Planets orbiting other stars outside our solar system.

- **GALAXY:** A massive cluster of stars, planets, and other matter held together by gravity.

- **GRAVITY:** The force of attraction all bodies of mass in the universe possess. The larger the body, the more gravity it has.

- **HELIUM:** A colorless, odorless gas that is the second lightest and the second most abundant element in the universe.

- **HUBBLE CONSTANT:** An equation that uses the speed of light to calculate the expansion rate of the universe.

- **HUBBLE SPACE TELESCOPE:** NASA's first orbiting observatory, placed in orbit above Earth's atmosphere in April 1990. It has been called the greatest scientific instrument of all time.

- **HUBBLE'S LAW:** The statement that the distance between galaxies and clusters of galaxies is continuously increasing and therefore the universe is expanding.

- **HYDROGEN:** A colorless, odorless gas that is the lightest and most abundant element in the universe.

- **HYPOTHESIS:** A proposed scientific explanation based on observation.

- **INTERNATIONAL SPACE STATION:** Orbiting scientific laboratory launched in 1998 and constructed and managed by the United States, Canada, Japan, Russia, the eleven nations of the European Space Agency, and Brazil. At any given time, two to three astronauts live on the space station for up to six months, doing research and conducting experiments.

- **JAMES WEBB SPACE TELESCOPE:** A space telescope that will be launched in 2014.

- **LAW:** In science, a general statement that describes regularly repeating facts or events.

- **LIGHT-YEAR:** The distance light travels in a year, about 6 trillion miles.

MATTER: Any substance in the universe that takes up space and has mass; matter can be liquid, solid, or gas.

MILKY WAY: The galaxy that is home to Earth's solar system.

NEBULA: An interstellar cloud of gas and dust.

OBSERVATION: In science, the act of watching and studying the behavior of an object or phenomenon over a period of time.

OBSERVATORY: A building or structure that houses equipment to study the stars, planets, and other celestial objects. Space telescopes such as the Hubble Space Telescope and the James Webb Space Telescope are frequently referred to as observatories.

ORBIT: The curved path one object takes as it revolves around another.

PLANCK TIME: The first measurable moment of the universe. Written as 10-43.

PLANET: A large, round celestial body that occupies its own orbit around a star and has cleared the neighborhood around its orbit of other bodies.

PROTOPLANETARY DISK: The leftover material from a star's formation that forms into a disk orbiting its star. Planets can be formed from these materials.

PROTOPLANETS: A small celestial object roughly the size of a moon, formed from dust and other particles that have collided and stuck together. Some protoplanets continue to gain mass until they form planets.

ROBOTIC ARM: A boom attached to the space shuttle.

SHUTTLE: A reusable space plane used for carrying astronauts and cargo between Earth and space.

SINGULARITY: An incredibly hot, dense point of matter, to which the laws of physics no longer apply.

SOLAR SYSTEM: A star and the collection of planets and other bodies that orbit it.

SPACE: The part of the universe beyond Earth's atmosphere.

SPACE TELESCOPE SCIENCE INSTITUTE: The Space Telescope Science Institute, or STScI, is responsible for administering the scientific work done with the Hubble Space Telescope and with the new James Webb Space Telescope.

SPACEWALK: Activity astronauts conduct in space while outside a space shuttle or the International Space Station.

SPECTRUM: A continuum of color formed when white light is broken into its component colors, or wavelengths.

SPEED OF LIGHT: Approximately 186,000 miles per second.

STAR: A celestial body that shines through the release of energy caused by nuclear reaction.

SUPERNOVA: A stellar explosion that occurs at the end of some stars' life cycles and is extremely bright.

TELESCOPE: An instrument that uses lenses, mirrors, or a combination of lenses and mirrors to make distant objects appear larger and closer.

THEORY: A statement based on a hypothesis that has not been disproved after testing and is generally agreed to be true.

UNIVERSE: All existing things, including all matter and all energy, on Earth and in space.

FOR FURTHER READING

BOOKS

Fleisher, Paul. *The Big Bang.* Minneapolis: Twenty-First Century
Books, 2005.

Jackson, Ellen. *The Mysterious Universe.* Boston: Houghton Mifflin
Company, 2008.

L'Engle, Madeleine. *A Wrinkle in Time.* New York: Fararr, Straus
and Giroux, 1962.

Miller, Ron. *Satellites.* Minneapolis: Twenty-First Century Books, 2007.

Rhatigan, Joe, Rain Newcomb, and Greg Doppmann. *Out-of-This-World
Astronomy.* New York: Sterling Publishing, 2005.

Thomson, Sarah L. *Extreme Stars! Q & A.* New York: HarperCollins, 2006.

Wright, Kenneth. *Scholastic Atlas of Space.* New York: Scholastic, 2005.

WEBSITES OF INTEREST

Amazing Space *amazing-space-stsci.edu*

Astronomy Picture of the Day *antwrp.gsfc.nasa.gov*

Hubble Space Telescope *hubblesite.org*

James Webb Space Telescope *jwst.nasa.gov*

National Aeronautics and Space Administration *www.nasa.gov*

Star Child: A Learning Center for Young Astronomers
starchild.gsfc.nasa.gov

Far flung galaxies, captured by the newly repaired
Hubble. NASA/ESA, AND THE HUBBLE SM4 ERO TEAM

INDEX

NOTE: Page numbers in **bold type** refer to illustrations.

ACS (advanced camera for surveys), 12, 19, 48

Altman, Scott, 5, 16, **17**, 18

Ariel I, 10

astronomy, 21

astrophysics, 21

Atlantis, 16, **18**, 19–20, **20**, 33

atoms, 40

batteries, 12

Big Bang, 23, 24, 25, 27, 30

Big Bounce, 25

Big Crunch, 30

black holes, 31, 35

creation of, **34**, 43

definition of, 33

at M87 galaxy, 37

and stars, **34**, **36**, **37**

blue stars, **58**

Bojowald, Martin, 25

brown dwarfs, 42, **42**

Carina Nebula, **52**, 53

CHRX 73 (red dwarf), **42**

Clampin, Mark, 49

clusters, 29

CMBR (cosmic microwave background radiation), 27, **27**

Columbia, 15, 18

Copernicus, Nicolaus, 8

COS (Cosmic Origins Spectrograph), 12, 19, 43

cosmic egg, 23

cosmology, 21–22, 25

COSTAR (Corrective Optics Space Telescope Axial Replacement), 10, 14

Crab Nebula, **32**

Danly, Laura, 5

Dark Ages, end of, 59

dark energy, 4, 29–31

dark matter, **28**, 29–31

dust, space, 49

Earth:

atmosphere of, 9

contamination from, 53–54

escape velocity of, 33

gravity of, 31, 33

and solar system, 48

Einstein, Albert, 5, **22**, 23

Endeavour, 18, 20

escape velocities, 33

event horizon, 34–35

exoplanets, 48, 49–50

Feustel, Andrew "Drew," **17**, 18, 19

FGS (Fine Guidance Sensor), 12

filaments, 24

fireball, 24

First Light, 59

Fomalhaut, 48, 49–50, **49**

Freedman, Wendy, 25

galaxies, **1**, **25**, **28**

assembly of, 24, 59

and dark matter, **28**, 29

evolution of, **26**

far-flung, **62**, 63

M87, **36**, 37

M100, **10**

Milky Way, 8, 22, 39

movement of, 22, 26–27, 29–30

NGC 1300, **6**, 7

NGC 5194, ii, **iv**

NGC 5195, ii, **iv**

NGC 6397, 40, **41**

Small Magellanic Cloud, **11**

Galileo Galilei, 5, 8, **8**, 9

Ganymede, **9**

glossary, 60–61

Goddard Space Flight Center, 14

Good, Michael, **17**, **19**

gravity, 4, 30, 31, 33, 46

Grunsfeld, John, 16, **17**, **18**, 19, 53

gyroscopes, 12

helium, 24, 40

Hooker Telescope, 22

Hoyle, Sir Fred, 24

Hubble, Edwin, 2, 4, 22–23, **23**, 27

Hubble Constant, 23

Hubble's Law, 22

Hubble Space Telescope, 2, 4, **4**

    calibration of instruments on, 54

    impact of, 14, 25

    instruments aboard, 12, **13**

    launch of, 10

    maintenance of, 4–5, 10, **10**, 14,

        15–16, 19, 57

    orbit of, 33, **33**

    outgassing, 53–54

    robotic arm of, **19**

hydrogen, 24, 40

hypothesis, 8

    testing of, 9

James Webb Space Telescope, 59

Johnson, Gregory C., **17**, 18

Jupiter, 8, **9**

Kalas, Paul, 49

Kepler, Johannes, 8, 9

Laplace, Pierre-Simon, marquis de, 35

law, scientific, 9, 22

Lemaître, Georges, 23, **24**

L'Engle, Madeleine, *A Wrinkle in Time,*

    1–2, 24, 50

light-years, 23

Lippershey, Hans, 7, 8

main sequence, 39, 40

Massimino, Mike, **17**, 18, 19

McArthur, Megan, **17**, 19

Mercury, 43

Michell, John, 35

Mikulski, Barbara, 57

Milky Way, 8, 22, 37, 39

Moon, **5**, 33

nebulae, 40, **43**, 46

    butterfly-shaped, 54, **55**

    Carina Nebula, **52**, 53

    Crab Nebula, 32

    Orion Nebula, **38**, 39, 46, **47**

Newton, Isaac, 4, 8–9, 22, 23

nuclear fusion, 40, 43

observation, 8

orbits, 8, 33

Orion Nebula, **38**, 39, 46, **47**

Osten, Rachel, 57

outgassing, 53–54

Penzias, Arno, 27

Perlmutter, Saul, 31

Piscis Australis, 48

Planck, Max, 24

Planck time, 24

planetesimals, 46

planets:

    characteristics of, 48

    discoveries of, **48**

    formation of, 24, 45–46

    orbits of, 8, 9, **51**

Pluto, **57**

Primeval Atom Hypothesis, 23

primordial fireball, 24

prisms, 9

protoplanetary disk, 46, 48–49, **49**

protoplanets, 46, 59

quarks, 24

radiation, 24, **27**

red dwarfs, 42, **42**

red giants, 42–43

relativity, theories of, 22

Riess, Adam, 30–31, **30**

scientific law, 9, 22

SI C & DH (Science Instrument Command
   & data handling module), 12

singularity, 23, 24, 25, 34

solar system:

   Earth and planets, 48

   formation of, **44**, 45

   Sun as center of, 8

Southern Fish, 48

spacetime, 35, **35**

speed of light, 23

spherical aberration, **10**

spyglass, 7

star factories, 40

stars, 2, **3**

   birth of, 24, 46, 59

   and black holes, **34**, **36**, **37**

   blue, **58**

   cluster of, 54, **56**

   intermediate-mass (red giants),
      42–43

   life cycle of, 39–40

   low-mass (red dwarfs), 42, **42**

   main sequence of, 39, 40

   in Milky Way, 8, 39

   nebulae, 40, **43**, 46, **47**

   neutron, 34, 43

   in NGC 1300, **6**, 7

in NGC 6397, 40, **41**

in Orion Nebula, **38**, 39

planets orbiting, **51**

Sun as, 43

supernovae, 30–31, **32**, 33, **42**, 43

twinkling, 9

types of, 42–43, **42**

very high-mass, 43

very low-mass (brown dwarfs), 42, **42**

white dwarfs, 42, 43

STIS (Space Telescope Imaging Spectrograph),
      12, 19

STS-125, 16, **17**, 18, 53, 59

STScI (Space Telescope Science Institute), 14, 59

Sun, 8

   age of, 43

   and spacetime, **35**

   as star, 43

supernovae, 30–31, **32**

   explosion of, 31, 33–34, **42**, 43

telescope:

   improvements in, 8, 9

   invention of, 7

   mirrors in, 9, **10**, 14

theories, 9, 22

time, 26

Tracking and Data Relay Satellite, **14**

universe:

   age of, 24–25, **26**, 27

   expanding, 22–26, 29, 30–31

Weiler, Edward, 57

WFC3 (Wide Field Camera 3), 12, 43

Wheeler, John, 33, **34**

white dwarfs, 42, 43

White Sands, New Mexico, 14

Wilson, Robert, 27

Zwicky, Fritz, **30**